Rise with Him

Rayanne Bedlan

Rise with Him

The untold story of a girl who finds Jesus

Rayanne Bedlan

Woodward & McCullough

"I would rather be a fool knowing I lived for God than to be wise in your eyes doing things for my own comfort"

- Stephanie Ike Okafor

Contents

Acknowledgments

This book would not have been possible without the support, encouragement, and guidance of so many people. However, first and foremost, I would like to thank God. I never thought it would be possible for me to write a short story, let alone publish a book! I was diagnosed with dyslexia and dyscalculia from a very young age, this made it incredibly hard to learn at the same rate my peers were learning at.

I worked incredibly hard all with that one goal in mind, get as many people as possible to like me so I will feel accepted by man. I am going to share a story with you about why I chose to even write this book. It was the summer of my senior year of high school, and I was confused on what my next steps in life were going to be. I had just dedicated my life to the Lord, and I really didn't know what I wanted to do. I was in prayer one day and I just simply asked the Lord: "What do you want me to do?" I thought he would tell me where I should go to college, what I should major in, how I would pay for it? However, He didn't answer in any of the ways I thought he would. Instead, he said: "I want you to write a book, but it can't be about you it has to be about me." I was shocked; how was I supposed to write a book when I have dyslexia, it didn't make sense. I sat on what God had said for 3 days, and I told God if this is really what you want me to do then tell me in 3 days again that you want me to write a book. Sure enough, God came back again on the third day and said, "I want you to write a book." This time I couldn't ignore it, I had to do what God had commanded, I had to write a book. So, I sat down at my computer and started to write. A couple days after I read back what I had written the previous day, I realized something, I didn't remember writing what

I had written the previous day. I asked God: "Why do I not recall writing this paragraph?"

God said: "Because I'm using you as a vessel, yes, your name will be on the cover, but the Holy Spirit will be the one who wrote the book through you."

This book would not be possible without the partnership of the Holy Spirit, so thank you Holy Spirit.

I also would like to thank my family for their unwavering love and patience. As well as my editors; this book was a challenging project for me, and having strong editors to help me along the way was truly a blessing.

I also would like to extend a well needed thank you to all my friends who supported me along the way. The love and support that every single one of my friends showed during this process was better than anything I could have asked for.

I am also very grateful to my publishing navigator who helped make this book possible. Phil Whitmarsh helped me publish a book I never thought would be published in a million years, so thank you. Also thank you to Phil's team at Redbrush for working alongside me throughout this entire process.

Finally, to all the readers who will pick up this book: I hope it speaks to you in ways both expected and unexpected. Your support, whether through a kind word or simply your interest, is what makes this journey worthwhile.

Thank you all from the bottom of my heart.

Chapter 1 – The Fear

We all deal with fear, whether big or small. We all have that queasy stomach when it comes to doing something we are not sure about or unfamiliar with—those times when we never really know what is going to happen next. However, this fear we feel is not something we have to live in. It is not something we are bound to have for the rest of our lives, and it is not something that has to define our life. Fear has the ability to wrap its chains around us, but we have the ability to break those chains. So, you might be asking yourself, why am I writing about fear in the first chapter of this book when this book is not called fear? Well, it is because fear is not only a part of learning how to be fearless but is also a part of how to rise up past that fear and become a new creation within Jesus Christ.

Before I start to dive deep into the meaning of fear, I would like to ask you a question first. Why do we fear things that we know God has control over? If we know that it is in God's hands and that he will take care of whatever it is we fear, then why do we fear it? The only way for me to explain this simple but at the same time confusing question is through the words of God himself. Psalms 46:1–3 says this: "God is our refuge and strength, an ever-present help in trouble. Therefore, we will not fear, though the earth gives way, and the mountains fall into the heart of the sea, though its waters roar and foam and the mountains quake with their surging." We by our own power cannot overcome the fear that surrounds us every day, but what we can do is trust that God takes this fear on his shoulders, so we don't have to carry it alone. We fear things we know God has control over, because we don't trust Him. We don't trust Him to be our refuge and strength, we don't trust Him to be our ever-present help in trouble. God wants to take our fear and put it on his plate, so that we don't have to go through it alone, God wants you to trust Him with your fear.

In Psalms 46:1–3 God says that even though this earth gives way, and we might be afraid of what may come next as the world starts to fall apart. We shall not fear worldly things but trust that He has the power to not only overcome the worldly disasters we can see but also the mental disasters that we can't always see. Sometimes I think we as humans forget that God is not only in control of the big things but the small things as well. Sometimes we look at God as the God who created the universe, the God who is all-powerful, and the God who never sins. Which you're not wrong, all of these statements about God is correct. However, we forget to look at God as the one who came down to earth and became like man, shared in our suffering so we don't have to endure suffering forever. Or we miss the chance to see God as our friend. We see God as this powerful being that we can't even confront because He is so powerful. Who am I to talk to God, who am I to ask Him for help? He won't help me because He's too busy. He's more focused on helping those who are living a godly life than a person who is not. These are lies, and not only are these lies, but they are lies the enemy whispers to try to get you to fall away from God.

God is never too busy for you; He is all-powerful, and if He is all-powerful, then He can be in two places at once. He can be helping you while also helping kids who are starving or kids who don't have a roof over their heads. So, is God in control of our mental health that we struggle with? Of course he is. He created our mind, and He knows us inside and out; so, don't fear that God is not walking with you as you go through mental health issues, or you experience a hurricane, but rather trust that He is with you instead of trying to carry it on your own.

Nothing is too big for God, nothing can take God down, and so if nothing can take him down, we should not fear that he won't be there for us. He will always be there in the big and small moments, amid your fear and amid your joy. He will be there covering you with his arm and saying to you, "So do not fear for I am with you, do not be dismayed for I am your God. I will strengthen you and help you. I will uphold you with my righteous right hand" (Isaiah 41:10).

Hi, I'm Rachel, and I have a lot of fear wrapped up inside of me and around me every single day. However, I also have a God, who is inside of me and outside of me protecting me and showering me with His love, kindness, hope, joy, and peace every day. I have a God who has changed the course of my life, and I want to share with you the life that I had before I met God, and the life that I have now, walking with God.

Chapter 2 – Change

You walk through those doors, and you realize you are not the same person you were back then than you are now. You see things have changed and for better. Well, you aren't sure. You don't know whether it's just your mind playing tricks on you or if you truly are excited about what this new life has for you. So, you sit somewhere that looks familiar to you, something you know and something that you don't have to figure out how to do. You sit next to your friends you have known since first grade. They know you, and you know them. They love you, and you love them. You spend time with each other and don't question whether things have changed. Sure, you haven't seen them all summer, but they haven't changed. They are the same now as they were back then, your friends. As we walked to class, my friends started to talk about all the new and exciting things that high school would bring them. It isn't like middle school, they said it's different and new.

You get to do and be so much more than you were in middle school, they all said. At the time I thought, *wow, this is great. I get more freedom than I did in middle school. I get to be a new invention of myself. The old is gone, and I am a new, fun, and exciting high school girl.* What could possibly go wrong? Once the bell rang, me and all my friend's parted ways. As I walked into history class, I sat in the back row hoping I would blend into the crowd. Most of the students in this class I knew from the previous year. There were a few here and there I didn't recognize, but other than that I knew most of my classmates. The tardy bell rang, and the teacher entered the classroom.

He had a textbook in his hand and a long green tie hanging down from his neck that said "Change" in big bold dark green letters. My eyes were fixated on that one word, "change." You know in the Bible they talk about change and what it means to live and grow from change. James 1:23–24 says this: "Anyone who listens to the word but does not do what it says is like someone who looks at his face in a mirror and, after looking at himself, goes away and immediately forgets what he looks like." Change is hard especially when it is a change that you necessarily don't want to make. All my friends said that changing from middle school to high school was going to be fun and exciting. "This is a good change, don't worry, just have fun with it..." my friends would say. However, I was worried, and I started to think about what it meant to truly change, and I didn't want to change. I liked middle school, why did I have to change? I was hearing what everyone was saying, but I was looking at my face in this mirror, and all I could see was my old self. My middle school self didn't want to jump into something that she wasn't familiar with. I preferred to stay in the shallow end of the pool because if I ventured into the deep end, anything could happen—I might even drown. Now as you can see this is a metaphor, I wasn't physically drowning in a pool, but I was mentally drowning in the fear of change. I wasn't going to do something that could possibly put me in danger!

Every time I looked at my teacher all I could see was that big green tie—a constant reminder that change, whether I like it or not, was going to happen—and all I wanted to do was crawl up in a shell and go back to my old life. Once the bell rang, I met my friends in the hallway. Half of them enjoyed their first-period class, and the other half complained about the teachers and how it was so unfair to give them homework on the first day of school. However, all I could think about was that green tie and James 1:23–24 and before even thinking, I said to my friends, "Why does God want us to change?"

Immediately after I said this, I felt instant embarrassment. Why would I say such a thing to people who generally love change? The group went quiet, and then Jamie looked at me with a look of confusion on her face. "God doesn't want us to change; he wants us to have fun, and change is fun." Then right at this moment, the bell rang, and we all went our separate ways. Before going to class I stood in the hallway for a minute at least, just in total shock about what Jamie had said. Is that all God wants for us to do? Does he just want us to have fun? He creates us just to have fun and not worry about what comes next? It didn't make sense to me; none of it made sense. Why was my teacher wearing a green tie that said "change" on it? Why do my friends find change so easy, and all I can see is the hardship that comes with change?

Chapter 3 – Faith

The next morning, I didn't feel like going to school; I wasn't mentally exhausted from being at school for only one day, but I did feel physically ill. So, my mom checked my temperature and said I had a 100-degree fever, so she wanted me to stay home from school. As I lay there in my bed feeling so sick I could barely move; my phone started to ring. My first reaction was just to let it ring, and I could call whoever it was back later. After about five seconds I lost my patience and had to answer the phone. I couldn't even last five seconds without checking my phone, I was that addicted to it. So, I stumbled out of bed and answered the phone; and Jamie was on the other end. I thought it was odd that she was calling me at 8 a.m. because usually she is not a morning person. I picked up the phone and right as I did, Jamie's little brother was on the other end. "Rachel!" he said in a loud, obnoxious voice.

"Jamie wanted me to call you and see if you are coming to school today?"

"I'm not coming to school; I'm sick," I said coughing.

"Oh OK; well, she says she is coming over to your house after school for an especially important conversation," Jamie's brother said, and then right after he was done speaking, he hung up the phone.

"Well, I don't want her…." I said as Jamie's brother hung up the phone. I didn't want Jamie to catch the cold that

I had; so, I called my mom into the room and asked her whether she could call Jamie's mom. I'd thought it would be easier for her just to tell Jamies mom instead of me having to argue with Jamie about it. This next sentence that my mom told me changed my life forever; as you know by now, I hate change. This is the day I found how to change positively for not only myself but for those around me as well.

"Jamie's mother passed away this morning," Mom said with tears in her eyes. I was in shock; my eyes started to fill with tears, and my mouth dropped so wide open I believe it touched the ground. The next thing I knew I was on the ground sobbing and my mother's arms wrapped around me.

"How could God let this happen!" I screamed hoping for an answer, looking for any logical reason why God would do such a thing. As my mom rocked me in her arms, she whispered this: "Rachel, because of the sin in this world it is broken, and terrible things will happen; however, because God is in control, He takes this brokenness and will use it for good. He will take this terrible thing that happened to Jamie's mom and use it to display His glory on this earth. It may be hard for us to see now, but in His time, God will bring great beauty out of ashes."

As I sat there in my mom's arms, I thought to myself, *the faith my mom has to see that God will bring beauty even though there are ashes raining down right now, is something I admire. My mom has so much faith that she can see the rainbow on the other side of a storm.*

19

"Mom, can I ask you another question?" I said, wiping the tears from my face.

"Sure," Mom said.

"How do you have so much faith to see someone die and still trust that God is good?"

"Rachel, have you heard the verse 2 Corinthians 12:9?"

"No," I replied, pulling myself up off the ground and giving my full attention to my mom.

"It says that My grace is sufficient for you, for my power is made perfect in weakness." Sometimes we must go through tough times for God to build up our faith. We see in 2 Corinthians that God is telling Paul that His grace is fully capable of providing everything Paul needs to endure the tough times he was going through. You see God wasn't telling Paul that he wouldn't go through hard times; He was telling Paul that you will go through hard times, but yet I will provide for you in those hard times. You know Rachel my faith isn't strong because I go to church every day or because I read my Bible. These are things that help grow my faith, but my faith is not strong because of them. My faith is strong because when things go wrong, I don't back out. I fall into His arms and choose daily to follow Him, believe and trust in Him. Every morning, I wake up and I deliberately choose to say yes to whatever God is calling me to do that day. Faith is a choice, and you choose every single morning when you see that sunrise to follow God or not to follow Him. For example, I woke up this morning and heard Jamies Mom passed away. I could have chosen to be angry at God, I could have been very bitter towards Him, but I wasn't, and you know why?" My mom asked as her face lit up so bright she looked like a lightbulb.

"Why?" I said, curious to see what she was going to say next.

"Because I knew He did this for a reason, so instead of choosing to be angry about things I can't see. I chose to have faith, even when I don't understand why He does what He does. This morning, I chose to bring Him all my sadness, anger, and fear; I laid it down at His feet and that was a choice only I could make."

Chapter 4 – Prayer

The next morning, I was feeling much better, and so I decided to go to school. I crawled out of bed and got ready for school; it wasn't until I walked out my front door that I realized that I was going to school to see my friends. Not only was I going to see my friends, but I was going to see Jamie. I had a whirlwind of questions and emotions racing through my mind. What was I going to say? What were my other friends going to say? I can't cry because if I do cry, then I can't be fully there for Jamie. All these terrible thoughts ran through my head; I couldn't get them out; they continued to fill my body with fear and anxiety.

Who are you to comfort Jamie in this time? You never lost a mom! Just go back home pretend you are sick today, so you don't have to deal with this! Just stop trying to be a good person!

"STOP!" I shouted so loudly that the neighbors across the street heard me. Embarrassed, I ran to my car and shut the door. I needed to be alone, away from all this noise that was surrounding me. However, I couldn't get away from this fear that was filling my body, so I folded my hands and prayed: "God, I don't know if you are listening or if you even care, but I feel this fear rising up in me, and I just need you to take it away. Take it out of me and let me live not in fear but in joy Lord. I don't want to feel like this, and I need your grace and your love to take this darkness out of me and put your love in. I'm scared to talk to Jamie. What if I mess it up?

What if I say something wrong and we are no longer friends?"

Before I could even finish my prayer, I heard something say, "Stop saying, 'What if' and start saying, 'I can do all things through Christ, who strengthens me."

At this moment I looked up to the sky, unfolded my hands, and looked around to see whether anyone else heard what I heard. There was no one in sight; I was in my car, windows rolled up, still sitting in my driveway, amazed by what I had heard. Not only was I amazed but I had heard but I was also in shock. I had never heard anything like it, a voice that felt unnatural, and it spoke to me! It was as clear as day, it wasn't my conscience speaking to me, it wasn't another human, it wasn't even the dog in my neighbor's front yard barking at me. It was real! As I started my car and drove off to school, all I could think about was how real that voice I heard felt.

Once I arrived at school all my friends were gathered around Jamie hugging her, crying over her, and saying to her, "It will be OK … if you need anything, I'm always here … we will get through this together."

I walked up to my friends and put a hand on Jamie. She was in tears, her eyes were swollen red and filled with sorrow, fear, sadness, and disbelief that things would get better. She looked up at me and didn't say anything; she just sat there. I sat next to her and wrapped my arm around her.

"Can I pray for you, Jamie?" I asked, she nodded her head, and all my friends gathered around her. I was hoping that the voice I heard this morning would show up and speak to Jamie. She was the one who needed that supernatural voice telling her that things would be OK. However, nothing happened; we all prayed for her to find joy, love, and peace again. We prayed that she and her family would be protected by God and that He would put His hand on them in this challenging time. We prayed, prayed, and prayed some more, but there was no voice; no light shined down on Jamie, nothing. Once we were done praying, I asked Jamie whether she had heard a voice or not.

"A voice? I heard you all praying for me, but I don't know what you mean by a voice," Jamie said with confusion on her face.

"So, you didn't hear anything at all?" I said hoping that she would change her answer.

"No. Rachel why are you asking if I heard a 'voice.' I didn't hear anything," she said putting fake air quotations around the word "voice."

I was shocked, why didn't God speak to her like He did to me? I thought about this all day. Why wasn't God speaking to the one who needed to hear Him the most? Once I got home my mom asked me how my day was. "Fine," I said brushing her off and heading immediately to my room. A few seconds later my mom walked into my room.

"What is wrong?" she said with her mother's intuition flashing a big red light over my head.

"I prayed for Jamie, and nothing happened, God didn't speak to her! I'm not the one who needs to hear God's voice; Jamie does!" I said frustrated at God.

"Honey," Mom said sitting down next to me on my bed. "God connects with everyone unique ways, because we are all different people. He spoke to you because you are different from Jamie, and maybe you needed to hear God's voice more than Jamie did. Proverbs 3:5–6 says "To trust the Lord with all your heart and lean not on your own understanding. In all your ways, submit to him and he will make your path straight." Honey, I think you are trying to understand God in a way that most of the world sees Him. In other words, you are seeing God as an all-powerful deity, and if we pray, He will fix our problems right away; but that is not always the case. God spoke to you, yes, but that doesn't mean He will heal Jamie's pain immediately. He might not speak to you the same way He speaks to Jamie and that is ok. God made everyone in his image, so this means that He will connect to each and every one of us in different ways. If you just lean into what God is truly saying, cancel out all the worldly desires that you have and focus on God's plan for you. You might find that He is listening to not only you, but He is also seeing Jamie and her needs as well," Mom said.

After mom was done talking to me, she left the room, and I was not sure what to do next. I laid in my bed for a long time thinking about what my mom said; then I decided to call Jamie. I picked up the phone, and it rang for quite a while until someone finally answered the phone.

"What do you want, Rachel?" Jamie said annoyed.

"I know what I said this morning did not help anything; it actually made things a lot worse. However, I wanted to say this: I was praying this morning asking God to help me find the strength to talk to you about your mom, and to be honest I was scared. However, now I know what to say. God told me to stop saying, 'What if' and start saying, 'I can do all things through Christ, who strengthens me.' I know it is hard losing your mom, and I know you are probably thinking, 'What if she still was alive? What if I was there when she died? Maybe I would have been able to save her.' Jamie, stop focusing on the what-ifs and start leaning into Him."

Chapter 5 – Father

It was Saturday morning, no worries in the world; I didn't have to focus on getting up and going to school, or what homework I had to do. I was completely free from school life at this very moment, and I couldn't feel more alive. I slept in till 10 a.m., and I could have slept even longer, but my mom came in and woke me up.

"Honey, time to get up; we have a big day today," she said in a cheery voice.

I rolled over in my bed pulling my covers over my head pretending not to hear her. However, she knew right away that I was faking being asleep because the next thing you know she was pulling me out of bed by my feet.

"It's a Saturday, what could I possibly have to do?" I complained.

"Your father is coming back from Israel!" Mom said as she left the room.

"WHAT!" I said jumping up in excitement. I hadn't seen my father for two years now! How was he going to act toward me, and better yet how was I going to act towards him?

Now, you might be asking yourself why my father was gone for such a long time in a foreign land. Well, after my mom and dad divorced, my father wanted to go back to his hometown, and that just happened to be Jerusalem. I had an option to stay in the USA or go to Israel; witch of course

Israel would have been fun but only for a few months. After a few months I would have wanted to go back home and see my friends. So, Mom kept me in the USA, and Dad went back home; I still would call my dad every night on Facetime just to see how he was doing. However, the reason I am so nervous to see him is because life is different seeing someone online than in person. I hadn't seen my dad physically in person for two years now, and the last thing he told me over Facetime was, "Love you." He never said anything about coming back to the USA.

I eventually crawled out of my bed and got ready for the day. Mom told me Dad's plane would be arriving around midnight tonight; good thing I slept in a little bit this morning so I would have enough energy to see my dad arrive in the lovely state of Minnesota. I lived in one of the biggest cities in Minnesota called Rochester, which held about 120,000 people.

As the day progressed, I got increasingly anxious about my dad's arrival. My mom cleaned the house all day, and when I say all day, I mean getting up at 6 a.m. and didn't stop cleaning until 9 p.m.

"Honey, I'm finished cleaning, so why don't we watch a movie until your father gets home." Mom suggested. I was all for it but only five minutes into the movie Mom passed out cold. I tried to wake her up, but she was sleeping so hard I could probably bring a mariachi band into the house and have them play as loud as they could, and she still wouldn't wake up.

I sat there for a good hour just twiddling my thumbs so nervous for my own father to walk through that door; why was I so nervous for my father whom I have known since birth to walk through that door? Well, it is because I truly didn't know him from birth; my father moved away when I was 12, and I am 14 now, and things have changed. Yes, I talk to my father a lot over Facetime, but I don't tell him everything, and he doesn't tell me everything either. We are two different people: what if he just treats me like I'm 12 because that's who he remembers me as?

As I sat there and worried about all the things my father was going to do, say, and be when he got here; the movie that my mom started caught my eye. It was called *God Is Not Dead*. As I watched this movie this kid who was only 19 years old believed so strongly in his savior that he was willing to fight against his professor for a potential failing grade to prove to not only his teacher but his class that God is real! He lost a relationship with his girlfriend, and his parents didn't want to get in the middle of what he was doing so they distanced themselves from their own son. His professor did everything in his power to disprove what this kid was saying and instead of giving up, he persisted despite every relationship he lost. Everything he knew he believed in so strongly that he was willing to go to the ends of the earth if he had to, to prove that God was real. Now if I have a God in heaven who is willing to do everything in his power to love me just like this boy did everything in his power to prove that God is real. Then why am I worrying about what my earthly father will think of me, when I already have a Heavenly Father who loves me so much!

So, yes, I am sitting on a couch waiting for my earthly father to show up after two years and hug me. However, I am also sitting here knowing that I have a Heavenly Father who will never leave for two years, two days, or even two seconds because that father is better than any father I could ever ask for.

Chapter 6 – Give Thanks

It was three days after my dad had returned to America, my mom and I had a wonderful time touring him around Minnesota, showing him various tourist attractions. We spent time shopping, which I obviously enjoyed, and not only did we do tons of fun things with my dad, but I also had the chance to get to know him better. He told me this story while he was in Jerusalem about this boy he met. The boy's name was Adam, he was a short dark-skinned boy with dark black hair. He never made eye contact with my dad; however, he loved to play football or as Americans would call it soccer. Every night Adam would invite his friends to come and play football with him and my dad. My dad even tells a story about how these boys stayed up till midnight playing football like there was no tomorrow.

One night after they played a couple of games of football this little boy came up to my dad and asked him whether he had a family or not. My dad replied with, "Yes, I do." Then the boy asked my dad whether he loved his family or not. Of course, my dad said yes, but as the word yes slipped off my dad's tongue the little boy looked up at him with these big brown eyes. This was the first time my dad saw this boy look him in the eyes.

"You know, there is a family I know who loves one another," the boy whispered. My dad knelt down to hear what the boy was saying, and the boy moved closer to my dad, whispering softly in his ear, as if the world would explode if anyone else heard what he was saying.

"My mother thinks I'm a burden, and my father told me that I'm like a grain of sand, amounting to nothing. My twin brother died when I was four, and my little sister was shot and killed by the Taliban. My grandma and grandpa live in the United States, as do my cousins, just like you, the boy said excitedly. I don't have any family who loves me, but do you know who does love me? The Messiah. I think the Messiah loves me so much that he sent you to play football with me. I prayed every day for the Messiah to give me a father to play football with, and I think he answered my prayers. I believe that if someone prays with their heart, the Messiah sees their faith and trust. Once he sees that, he tells the angels to send someone to me, and they sent you," the little boy whispered.

As the little boy finished talking, my dad said, "I looked him straight in the eye, and I didn't see a little boy anymore. I saw a person who had prayed for seven years, and finally, he saw that his prayers had been answered. He had so much faith in the Messiah that he was willing to look another man in the eye, which is not well-received in the Islamic religion. He broke the rules he grew up learning to see the gift he had been praying for."

As I was taking in this story that my dad was telling me, I remembered a story in the Bible about a woman named Hannah. She wanted to have a son so badly that she prayed to God to give her a son. Her first prayer she prayed was bitter. However, God still heard her prayer, and soon after this prayer, she gave birth to a son.

This son she named Samuel because the name Samuel means "God has heard." Hannah recognized that God had heard her prayer, and the Bible says she rejoiced. She was so happy that God had granted her a son that she prayed giving thanks to God for giving her this son. This little boy that my dad met in Jerusalem, in a lot of ways, is similar to Hannah. He prayed for God to give him another person who would love him. God provided for him, and once he saw that, he gave thanks to God for answering his prayer.

Once my dad was finished telling this amazing encounter with this boy, he had in Jerusalem he said this: "Darling, I think along the way I find myself praying for God to answer my prayers, and once he does, I don't thank him enough for answering it. It is like getting a Christmas present: You ask for one specific gift all year, and finally, Christmas rolls around, and you get your gift. However, you don't say thank you to those who gave it to you. You get so caught up in what it is and how it will benefit you that you never stop and thank the person who made it possible for you to have this gift. This little boy not only saw the gift, but he saw the giver as well."

Chapter 7 – The Door

It has been officially six whole months with my dad, and these last six months were amazing! Laughing with him, seeing him smile, hearing and learning all kinds of stories this man had. I truly learned so much from him in these six months than I ever had in the whole two years he was gone. However, every great adventure has its end, and it was time for my adventure to end. My dad was officially going back to Jerusalem and was excited to see his parents again but was sad to leave me and Mom. We didn't have any exciting "going back home party" for him, we just said our goodbyes and watched him leave.

As he hopped in the taxi, I didn't feel the same as I did when he first left. Despite the fact that he was leaving the first time because my parents had gotten a divorce when I was 12, I also felt bitter toward my dad. I hated him for leaving me and Mom all alone. I didn't understand it, but I had found a new grace and appreciation for my dad. Even though he did leave, and it did suck, I wasn't mad at him anymore. I was actually proud that he was my dad. I no longer viewed him in this light as the man who hurt my mom and left me all alone. I saw him as a caring, loving, faithful father who all he ever wanted to do was love his family, and sometimes when you love someone you have to leave. My dad left so that my mother could live a happier life. He left so that I wouldn't have to grow up around parents who fought all the time. He did this because he realized that it wasn't working, none of the decisions he was making in his marriage or even in his life were leading him down a good path. He knew more than anything that something in him needed to change soon, or else things could get a lot worse not only for himself, but for his wife and child as well.

There is a verse in Proverbs and it says this: "We look to see where He is working or where He has called us, and we do the thing that lines our actions up with God's will, committing our plans to Him, and not just operating out of our own feeble understanding." You see, my father wasn't looking to line his actions up with any worldly possessions, plans, things, or ideas. However, he was using God as his moral compass; he saw that he couldn't fix his marriage even though he knew that it would hurt a lot to leave his family and start a new life. He also knew that God may have shut this door, but God is not done opening doors either. I also would like to point out that if my dad did not trust God and did not go to Jerusalem, then he would have never made all the wonderful memories he had. He wouldn't have connected with that little boy in such a profound way; he wouldn't have learned as much as he did while he was in Jerusalem. If God had not shut that marriage door for my dad and opened up a new door for him in Jerusalem, then he would not be the man he is today.

Sometimes I think we, as scared and fearful human beings, don't walk through that new door, because we are scared of what could be on the other side. Or we are content with what we are living in right now that we don't find a need to move through those doors.

In the Book of Revelations, it says, "For I am rich, I have become wealthy, and I need nothing, and you don't realize that you are wretched, pitiful, poor blind and naked." We all have those days where we just don't want to get out of bed. While rest isn't a bad thing, and God says that we should rest, that it is good for our soul. Too much of this rest and being happy with a lot of rest is not how we reach our full potential that God has for us. God has made us all to do well and thrive, no matter our circumstances; God gave you every resource you need to be successful on this earth. Now if God has given me everything I need to do well on this earth, why should I settle for less. Why do I just sit here and be content with staring at that door and not passing through it?

There is no doubt that we were made to do big things in this world, and we have. However, there are a lot of people who aren't like my dad. They don't pass through that door, and they stay in a marriage that is not only hurting them but those around them as well. They can't bear the thought of leaving because if they do leave then what will happen next? They are afraid of what may be on the other side of that door. There are also people who stay in a job they don't like, they stick with this job because even though it might not be their favorite thing to do, it gives them money and it helps provide for their family, so why change? As you can see in this type of situation the contentment is holding them back from passing through that door.

So there again, these people don't pass through this door because they don't feel a need to, or they're scared of what may be waiting for them on the other side. We can say all day long that we don't want to do something because it is scary, or that we don't want to do it simply because there is no need to change now. However, think about all the blessings that God wants to give you that you are missing out on when you say, "No, I'm not going through that door."

Chapter 8 – A Hard Heart

It was officially summertime of my senior year, and you know what that means: the time to let go of high school and focus on your future that is soon approaching. I prepared to have the best last summer with all my high school friends. I planned out sleepovers, trips we could take, games we could play, and so forth. I put all of these ideas into a document and sent all my friends two of them just in case they lost one, they would always have another. It took me two hours to make the document, and once I was finished, I hit send. It took my friends a good hour to respond to the document I sent them. However, once they did, it was like my world shattered into a million pieces.

Jamie: "I'm sorry, Rachel, but I got hired to work at Starbucks this summer, and I don't think I'll be able to hang out with you guys because I will be busy working. I need this money for college!!!"

Mia: "Wow, Rachel, looks like you put a lot of time into this, and I love it. However, I can't hang out with you in the month of June or July because my parents are taking me to Hawaii for 2 MONTHS!!!! Aloha!!!!"

Charlotte: "I think I can hang out on the first of June?"

Eleanor: "Rachel, I think you are an amazing friend, and I would love to hang out with you this summer, but me and my twin sister have decided to travel across the United

States this year. We plan to hit all 50 states before we both go off to college. Also, have you ever thought about being a secretary you're really good at organizing information."

Once I had finished reading all the messages, I felt my heart sink deep down into my stomach. Here I was thinking of how much time I would have with my friends before we all went our separate ways and lived our separate lives. It was almost like every single one of them didn't care about our last month's together. Did they even realize what this meant? Did they know that once August hits we will never see each other again? As I started to spiral down this whole sadness, fear, and loneliness slide my mom entered my room. I was curled up in a ball, lying on my bed sobbing as my mom entered my room.

"Darling, what is wrong?" she said, pulling the cover away from my face so she could see me.

"My friends are leaving me, and they don't even care that after August we won't be friends anymore." I cried dramatically.

"Oh, honey, I'm sure that is not true," she said, trying to cheer me up.

This just aggravated me more and I said, "Mom, you don't understand. You never had to go through losing your friends to college." I cried in a state of utter despair.

"Yeah, right, I didn't!" She laughed. "I went to high school just like you did, and I had lots of friends who I was going to miss dearly. I even had this one friend that I was so close with, we threatened our parents that we would glue our bodies together so then we would never be separated. However, this did not go over well with our parents, but that is beside the point. Honey, there are going to be times when you are going to have to leave people you have built relationships with, and you are going to have to find a way to move from these situations without losing your kind heart. Darling, you have a heart that is so generous, kind, patient, and loving. You may lose things in this life, but the ability to lose something and still hold on to your heart is something that people will admire. They are going to see a person who they want to be friends with because that person's heart is something they want to be around. I know it is hard leaving your friends, but don't be bitter toward them. Because being mad at them will only make your heart harden faster. Your friends will always be there; even when you are miles away. You will find new friends while also being able to stay connected with your old friends through Facetime, social media, and so many other amazing apps that help you stay connected with others."

My mom gave me a big hug and put her lips to my forehead. Once her lips reached my forehead, I knew that even though my friends may be going away, I have a mom who believes in me that I will make it. Having that person whether it be a parent, friend, or coworker; is so important, and I now realize that. Everyone needs that person who doesn't bring them down but lifts them up when they are uncertain. That person for me just happens to be my mom. She was absolutely right, I can either be angry at my friends, creating a heart that is bitter towards them, or I could choose to take this opportunity to love them, even though the time is short.

Chapter 9 – Everlasting Energy

"Did you know that water is so vital to our everyday life? Every time you take a drink of water it brings nutrients to your cells. It gets rid of the waste that builds up inside your body. It helps protect your joints and organs to function better, while also maintaining a good body temperature?" Mrs. Taylor said.

Then as the class continued, she went on to say this: "We have this thing that we are given for free, that will improve our bodies' function and help us live a healthier lifestyle, but somehow we find ourselves not drinking from the very thing that will give us a healthy life. According to the American Heart Association 30% of teens between ages 12 and 17 regularly drink energy drinks. The side effects of drinking these beverages are:

1. Dehydration: The number one thing that helps your body is being depleted from drinking these drinks.
2. Heart complications: These drinks speed up your heart, giving you a more likely chance to have heart problems in the future.
3. Anxiety: Philippians 4:6 says, "Do not be anxious about anything, but in every situation, by praying and petitioning with thanksgiving present your request to God." The very thing that God says not to do, we are inviting into are bodies.

4. Insomnia: The drinks have so much caffeine in them that falling asleep is very hard to do after drinking energy drinks. The nutrition labels even show 200 to 300 milligrams of caffeine are in one energy drink, says Ilisa Nussbaum, RD, a registered dietitian nutritionist at Yale Children's Hospital.

Mrs. Taylor continued to state the facts on why energy drinks are one of the most consumed beverages in the USA yet are one of the worst things we could drink. After informing us on the scientific side, she asked, "Why do the people in this world see something that will give them life but reject it for something that has a cooler color or something that will only give them temporary energy? Why are we so easily convinced that a drink that is so bad for our health is something we want to spend our money on?"

After 10 seconds of silence, Jim, a kid who sits in the back of the class and drinks an energy drink every day, a kid who ate potato chips for lunch and falls asleep during class every single day, answered the question. "Because it looks good to drink," he said proudly.

The whole class was in shock; they never even heard this kid talk, and here he was speaking in class! Even the teacher was surprised, Mrs. Taylor looked at Jim and smiled. Then she said, "Because it looks good, that is why we are so easily convinced to buy these energy drinks. Even though we know the terrible things that it does to our bodies, we do it because on the outside it looks good. In the same way, the enemy makes an apple look good on the outside to trick us into thinking that it is truly good on the inside. When in all reality it was a rotten apple all along, we just didn't realize it, because we were so fixated on the outward appearance. So, what do we do next? We take a bite out of that apple. Then we quickly find out that it is not what it seemed, we find that this apple is not of good but of evil. You see, our culture sees the water of life, but they revert to otherworldly things because on the outside the worldly things look like they will plenish our soul for eternity. The world sees the water, and they think, *oh, it doesn't look appealing, so I'm going to trade the everlasting well for something that looks more appealing to my eyes.* Mrs. Taylor explained that God is the everlasting well, but we don't search for Him because we see something that we think is better. We wonder why this energy drink is not giving us the energy we need to get through a year. Well, it is because this drink was not made to last you a year but only two days, and once those two days are up, you are right back to square one. However, if you search for not what looks good but the water that is so crystal clear; then you might just find that everlasting energy that will never run out. This energy will never fade, and it will fill your soul till it can't be filled anymore. Because that energy is not something you can find in a drink but an everlasting God.

Chapter 10 – Curveball

I laid in my bed thinking of all the things Mrs. Taylor said on our last day of school; what truths my mom had been whispering over me, and what my friends had been saying, as well as what my dad told me about his time in Jerusalem. It was summer, and next year I would go to college, or at least I thought so. However, the more and more I thought about going to college, the more I didn't want to go. I didn't know what I wanted to major in, or even if I wanted to learn more. High school was hard for me, nothing ever came easy for me, and it wasn't like I didn't try to do well in school; I did try; I tried really hard. Learning just didn't come easy for some reason. Most of my friends saw school as the next step, which for most people it was. Go to high school, make friends, do well in high school, and be involved. Then go to college, meet your future husband, find lifelong friends, and get a degree that satisfies you. Once you have done all these things get a job, settle down with your husband, and have a family.

This was normal, this is what the majority of people in Minnesota did and as a matter of fact the world followed this system as well. No one ever challenged this system because for a lot of people, it worked, but for some reason, I didn't want this "normal" that everyone talked about. I wanted something more, there had to be something more than this, something bigger than what everyone saw. As I started to think about what I genuinely wanted to do, I couldn't think of anything! What did I want to do with the rest of my life? This is a big question to ask an 18-year-old, but for some reason most 18-year-olds I knew seem to figure it out. They all seem to find their purpose; why can't I find mine? Do I really want to spend my whole life savings on a degree that I might not even use in my future? Do I really meet my soulmate in college, and what if I don't? What if I never find a man who loves me, and I end up graduating college and never have a family? What if I ended up living alone with 12 cats and a dog to comfort me. I don't want that for my future!

I couldn't stand these questions swarming my mind anymore, so I called Jamie. She would certainly know what to do. She is one of those friends who always knows what to say and how to say it.

"Hey, Rachel, what's up?" she said as she picked up the phone.

"Jamie! I don't know what to do with my life. I don't know if I want to go to college or if I even want to get married, but that is what everyone else is doing, and so what other choice do I have? I mean, look at you: you have your whole life planned out. Where you want to go to college, what you want to do as a career, and you have a boyfriend. I have planned out nothing except for a summer with my friends that didn't work anyway because everyone is so busy except for me. What should I do?"

I desperately needed an answer to anything that would point me to something better than what I was thinking then.

"Wow, Rachel, you thought about that for a long time, haven't you," Jamie said in shock.

"Yes, yes, I did. Now, Jamie, tell me what to do!" I cried.

"You know we all don't have to figure our lives out right now. Everyone is telling us we must have everything figured out. Which, yes, it would be helpful if we did have it all figured out, but we don't; none of us do. No one I know on this earth right now has their lives figured out. Even those of us who are in college or out of college. Life will always be changing, and new things will come that you may not know how to handle. The lie the world is tossing around is that you must have your life plan figured out before you go to college, which is false. You don't have to have anything figured out. In fact, I don't know what I'm going to do when I go to college at all. I think it would be fun to join a sorority, but I might get to college and figure out that sororities are not my thing and do something else instead.

"Our lives will always change and throw us curveballs that we didn't expect. Sometimes we will hit a curveball right into the green, but most of the time we won't see it coming and strike out. I know it is scary not know what is around the corner; I didn't know that my mom was going to pass away at such an early age; that was a curveball that I sure wasn't ready for. However, I have learned that even though these curveballs may hit me or strike me out, being able to shake it off and just do the next right thing in life, will get you farther in life than just running the bases because that is what everyone else is doing. Rachel, you're not everyone else; you are you. So go to college or don't go to college to find who you are as you battle life's curveballs. Now, I know that was really baseball oriented, and it is just because I got back from my little brother's baseball game, so sorry about that," Jamie said.

"Wow, Jamie, that was good! You know I really do appreciate you. Being your friend throughout high school had its ups and downs, but we always managed to work things out, and that strengthened our friendship. I really am going to miss all your good advice," I said, trying not to cry.

"Well, if you ever need me, I'm just a call away," she said, and then we hung up the phone. She was right in every single way; I don't know what I want to do with my life, but what I do know is that I will learn how to battle these curveballs with God by my side.

Chapter 11 – Forgiveness

It was officially June 20th, and it was an incredibly special day; not only was it my birthday, but it was the day my friends and I were going to hang out for the first time in an exceedingly long time. I had seen a couple of my friends separately throughout the summer so far but never all of us in one room. I woke up, brushed my teeth, washed my face, brushed my hair, put on my makeup, and prepared to have one of the best days of summer ever. Jamie told me it was going to be a surprise party, which I didn't mind because I hated surprises anyways so I'm glad she told me. Jamie and Charlotte were going to pick me up while Mia and Elenor were waiting at the special place to surprise me! I was so excited I could barely stand up straight. I walked into the kitchen to grab something to eat before I headed out, and there was my mom with a cake in her hand and candles lit up so brightly I could barely see the cake.

"Happy birthday, darling," Mom said with a smile so big I thought it was going to cover her whole face. Then she started to sing. "Happy birthday to you, happy birthday to you, happy birthday, dear Rachel, happy birthday to you." Mom sang as her eyes started to fill with water.

Then I heard a car horn: "Honk honk, Rachel, let's go, you don't want to be late for your birthday!" Jamie yelled from outside. I panicked, I looked at my mom, and I looked at my friends outside. "I love you, Mom, but I'll have to finish the cake later, I'm spending time with friends today," I said as I grabbed my bag and headed straight for the car. I knew my mom loved me; surely, she wasn't hurt by me not staying with her on my birthday. She also understood that I had friends, so she knew I needed to hang out with them on my birthday. Once I hopped in the car, I felt this deep cloud of fear come over me. I thought to myself, *what if me and my friends changed so much that we aren't going to be close friends anymore?* I couldn't let this rain cloud ruin my day, so I tried to silence these insecurities.

As I sat down in the passenger seat Jamie and Charlotte were playing my favorite song, and they weren't just playing my favorite song, but they had the volume pumped up so loudly the car was shaking. This was where I was meant to be on my birthday, right here with my friends. "Rachel! Are you ready for this? It will be the most epic day of your life!" Jamie said as she pushed on the gas, and instantly we flew off into the road.

Charlotte blindfolded me wrapping a piece of cloth around my eyes so I couldn't see where we were going. As Jamie drove to the mystery birthday place, I felt happy but also a lot of guilt for leaving my mom the way I did. She prepared a whole cake for me, and I didn't even say goodbye. However, I couldn't let this guilt ruin my day, I had to make the best of this day; it was my birthday, and what was there to worry about? Once we arrived at the mystery place my hands were shaking so hard, I could barely grip the door handle to get out of the car.

"OK Rachel, it's time to get out of the car," Charlotte said, helping me out of the car and guiding me toward the mystery place. I could hear Mia and Elenor in the background giggling, and as I pulled my blindfold off, I saw the words Putt-Putt Golf written in big letters across this building that looked like a castle.

I had loved going to Putt-Putt golf ever since I was a little kid, and my friends sure knew that because they brought me to the best Putt-Putt golf place in town: Can Can Wonderland in St. Paul.

"Thank you guys so much, you are the best friends I could ever ask for."

We spent the entire day from sunrise to sunset playing Putt-Putt golf. At the end of the night, we tallied up who won, and then we went back home. As Jamie drove me back home, she realized something was not right with me. So, she did as any good friend would do and asked the common questions of "What is wrong?". At first, I denied there being anything wrong, but she knew there was something not right about me.

"My mom made me this cake this morning, and I left it there for her to eat and I didn't even say goodbye. What kind of daughter am I? I just wanted you all to like me, I want you all to not have to worry about hanging out with me because you think I'm a burden…"

Just before I could finish Jamie interrupted me. "Where are you getting this idea that we don't want to hang out with you? Rachel, if we didn't want to hang out with you, we would tell you. Second, your mom loves you, and yes, it was rude to leave her like you did, but also if your mom loves you, she also can forgive you. That goes for any relationship: if you have a person who loves you, truly loves you, they will forgive you and continue to show you love. On the other hand, if you have a person who loves you but doesn't forgive you, then they truly don't love you enough to recognize you are human too and you make mistakes just like the rest of us. Sometimes it might take a person longer to forgive you, and you must accept that. Your mom loves you, Rachel, and she will forgive you. There is actually a Bible verse on forgiveness, and it says this: 'For if you forgive other people when they sin against you, your Heavenly Father will also forgive you.' Rachel, God forgave all our sins and just like God we are supposed to forgive others as well because that is what Jesus did as he laid on that cross and took up all our sins."

I knew Jamie was right, so I went in and told my mom I was sorry. God did fulfill his promise to forgive our sins, and my mom forgave me that night as I sat there begging for her forgiveness; she forgave not on her own understanding, but she did it because God forgave us. None of us are obligated to forgive anybody; however, when you think about believers in Christ, who are we supposed to be modeling in our day to day? If you answered with Christ, you are on the right track. Jesus' time and time again forgave his disciples, mother and even his enemies. We as Christians are supposed to be Minie Christs; forgiving even when it is hard. My mom probably didn't want to forgive me, and she had all the right to say "No I'm not forgiving you" but she didn't say that because she saw the importance of living out what you say you are. We can say all day we are Christians but if we don't forgive our neighbor than are we really a miniature representation of Christ?

Chapter 12 – Lies

Did you know that Children first start to learn the concept of what a lie is and how to lie by the age of two! Before most two-year-olds know how to tie their shoes they have already learned how to tell a lie. Then when they hit the age of 4, they start lying at a rapid passe. Studies have shown that 80% of children are already lying to keep the truth that they may have done something wrong, hidden from those who will most likely not approve of the wrong that this child has done. The crazy thing is this rapid lying starts when a child is only 4 years old! Lying is not an easy task, there are certain skills that a child learns at a young age to give them the ability to tell a lie. They must inhibit telling the truth, hold a working memory of what is true, and plan an alternative statement. It takes a lot of work to lie, but somehow children still tend to want to tell a lie instead of telling the truth; why is this? Why is telling a lie versus telling the truth for some reason something that we as children and even as adults desire more? Why are we so focused on convincing others of something false rather than just saying what truly happened?

John 8:44 says this: "You belong to your father, the devil, and you want to carry out your father's desires. He was a murderer from the beginning, not holding to the truth, for there is no truth in him. When he lies, he speaks his native language, for he is a liar and the father of lies." We were born not perfect but sinful because Adam and Eve ate from the tree of knowledge of good and evil. We did not choose this sin, but because of the disobedience that was shown in the garden that day, we automatically enter into sin the moment we are born. It is in our human nature to sin; it is in our human nature to want to follow our father of lies and that is the devil. As we see in John 8:44, the devil is the father, the head of sin and lies. We may be sinful human beings, but that does not mean we have to fall into this trap of lying. Lying is like a cycle; just like with anything in this world, good or bad, once you have done it one time, it is easier to do it a second time.

Jamie told me the other day that she was so excited to go skydiving again. This was her third time skydiving, and I asked her why she was so excited; wasn't she scared? She is going 10,000 feet off the ground into an airplane that will open its door, and once it does, you must make sure you do everything right, or else you might die. You must ensure your harness is secure, so when you jump out of the plane, you don't lose your parachute. You must prepare days in advance mentally and physically, also make sure to eat something before you jump so you don't get lightheaded and possibly pass out when jumping. You also need to wear a helmet just in case your landing doesn't go as planned! There are all kinds of repercussions and scary events that could possibly happen when skydiving. Why was Jamie not afraid to jump out of that plane? Why was she so calm?

She explained to me that it wasn't that she didn't know or believe that there were risks involved; she fully knew the risks going into it. However, she had also done it two times previously, so she wasn't as afraid or nervous to do it because she had done it before. In a comparable way, the more you lie, the easier and less scary it can be. As a child the first time you lie you are fearful of the consequences of getting caught. However, once you lie more and more, the easier and less scary it gets.

In the Ten Commandments, it says "You shall not give false witness against your neighbor." What this means is when we are giving information to others it should not be with a tongue of lies pouring out of it; but rather we should speak with a tongue that gives truth. Even though we are sinners, and it is in our nature to sin, it is also in our nature to tell the truth. To live not in communion with the devil or live a life of sin, but to live a life as a child who wants to do right by his or her Heavenly Father. We can choose to live a life following those who repeat the lies the enemy is whispering to them, falling deeper and deeper into this cycle of lies. Or we could choose to follow the Father who is not of lies but of truth. Who has sacrificed for us, so we don't have to live in a constant state of lies. Who has called us by name and knows the number of hairs on our heads. So, yes, lying is in our sinful nature, but we as children of God are not called to live in that sin day after day, but to recognize it and turn the other way. To continue to choose the way that is higher than our own understanding, to live for something that is only truth and not lies. To love one another and not hate one another for the lies they tell, but to show them there is a better way than to lie. We are called to rise above our sinful nature and be the best unperfect Jesus we can be. Because that is where truth comes from.

Chapter 13 – Love Others

If you don't already know, I basically grew up as an only child. I have an older brother, who moved out of the house when I was five, so I really didn't know him that well. His name is Zach, and I think he went to the University of Minnesota for college, but I'm not sure. His degree is in engineering, and he lives in Houston, Texas. I rarely see him in Minnesota; the last time I can remember him visiting us was two Christmases ago, and he was getting engaged to Jesica. However, after that Christmas, Mom and I had no contact with him. He never calls to tell us what is going on in his life now, and he never sends any pictures as well. I have tried to see whether he has any social media, and I can't find anything. One day I even tried looking him up on Google, but to no one's surprise, nothing popped up.

It is fine that he doesn't stay connected with me; I was five when he left, and so I never really had a connection with him, but when you lose total connection with your mother, that is a different story. The one who raised you, the one who rocked you to sleep every night and the one who took care of you, why wouldn't you stay in touch with an amazing person like that? I was raised by the same mother, and I can proudly say that my mom is the best mom of them all. I might be a little biased, but truthfully, who isn't when it comes to their own mother? All my other friends have brothers and sisters who are older than them, but those people never lost contact with their family. Most of them even come back for holidays and spend time with their mothers. I just have never understood why Zach did what he did. When I was 10 years old, I remember my mom praying for him even though she had no clue what he was doing or even where he was. She still prayed that he was in a good place, she prayed that he was kind and generous to others and she hoped that he loved his wife like a husband should.

I always thought it was so interesting that even when Zach had left her, and she had no clue what he was doing, she still prayed for him every night. She would ask God to protect him when she can't, and she prayed for him to have faith to stand up for what he believes in. I started to think about what my mom does for him even though he has moved out of the house, has lost contact with any of his biological family, and has hurt my mother. She sets aside all of these things I mentioned above and still prays for him. I admire my mom for many reasons, but one of the reasons I love my mom the most is her humility. She humbles herself so much that she will pray for those who don't seem to care about her anymore. My mom could have many distinct reasons to be angry at Zach. She could let her emotions get the best of her, and she would have the right to be angry at Zach for leaving her the way he did. However, she puts her anger and bitterness aside and instead prays that he is living a good life. It is not that she doesn't have these feelings, when she sees him for one Christmas and wants to tell him, "Hey why haven't you been talking to me for all these years?" No, she does have these feelings of anger and sadness for what he has done to her. The difference is she doesn't let it consume her. She knows that she could be angry when she sees him, but she also knows that God loves her and even loves him. So, she chooses to love him while he is here and while he is gone because God calls us to love others just as he loves us.

There is a Bible verse that I read the other day that reminded me of the love my mother has for my brother. Luke 6:27–29 talks about Jesus speaking to a crowd of people saying. "But to you who are listening I say: Love your enemies, do good to those who hate you, bless those who curse you, pray for those who mistreat you. If someone slaps you on one cheek, turn to them the other also. If someone takes your coat, do not withhold your shirt from them."

My mother is a full embodiment of what this bible verse truly means. My brother mistreated her, but she still prays for him. My brother hurt her and metaphorically slapped her across the cheek, and she still loves him anyway. My mom still sends Christmas cards to Houston, Texas, and even though my brother hurt my mom's heart, she still gives. Love can be a tricky thing, and it sure can be convincing when your close relatives and even your own son doesn't show you love back, to want to hurt them. However, when you have a teacher who is love himself, you learn a simple heart posture that will change your perspective. My mom puts her heart in a place of loving her son even when it is hard. By doing this she can live in freedom; she is not held down by the sadness of not seeing her son, she is not held down by anger of him not loving her back, she is not living in a state of regret for what she could have said or done to keep him around. She is set free by looking at her situations, acknowledging what has happened, but not letting herself stay there. She humbles herself just like Jesus did and prays for her son above herself.

Chapter 14 – Waiting on the Right Man

What is true love? I have never had a boyfriend, and in fact I have never even went on a dated with a man before. I haven't got married yet, and I am not planning on it anytime soon. I am 18 years old, and I have not had a boyfriend. This might seem shocking to most because lots of people start dating at a really young age. Although I myself have never been married or even dated anyone up to this point in my life, I have been to a lot of weddings in my lifetime. I remember the first wedding I went to; it was such a cute wedding; the couple was noticeably young, but that didn't stop them because what they had was love. We all gathered on the tennis court to witness this great love story, as they gave each other flowers that they each picked by hand, they sealed the deal with a plastic ring and a hug. Now you might be wondering what kind of wedding is this? It doesn't seem like a normal wedding to me, and if you are asking yourselves these questions, you are right. This is not a normal wedding; it is quite the opposite of a normal wedding. Two of my classmates in sixth grade wanted to get married because they "were in love."

As I stood there as a sixth-grade girl having no clue what was going on, I thought to myself, *how could a person at such a young age find love?* Now, this couple did not end up lasting for a long time, like most of the couples in sixth grade did anyway. Most of them found other interests, other hobbies, new people to hang out with, and so forth. However, this wedding did get me thinking about love a lot. As I got older, I started to go to more and more weddings that were not centered on a playground and using plastic rings to seal their marriage. They were adults who got to know each other over years of dating and found that they truly loved each other. They were getting married not because someone in their sixth-grade classroom told them they liked their watercolor painting, but because they enjoyed being around this certain person.

Marriage is a big thing; saying you will love someone through sickness and health and promising them you will be there for them no matter what life throws your way is a huge commitment. It doesn't always work for everyone either. As you can see, it didn't work for my parents, and it didn't work for my sixth-grade classmates either.

People ask me all the time: "Rachel how have you not had a boyfriend yet?" This is a valid question, and for a long time, I said, "I just never had any interest in getting a boyfriend," which is partially true: I never really had an interest in throwing myself into something that could possibly not work. I was so focused on school and being involved in school that I never really wanted to add anything more to my plate. It was not like I didn't want to get married and have kids. Yes, this is one of my desires, but it was not a top priority for me at the time. I saw the heartbreak that can come from a relationship not working out, and I really didn't want to put myself into that. I had no desire at all to get married for one day like that couple in sixth grade just to break up the next.

There is a lot about marriage and dating in general, wrapped up in the Bible as well. Most couples in the Bible even get married when they are around the age of 13 or 14. I knew what marriage was, and I knew what dating was; it wasn't as if I was oblivious to what it meant to date and what it meant to get married. However, giving your heart to someone else who could potentially use your own heart against you is a very scary thing to do. In high school I caused myself to get stressed over things that didn't need to be stressed about. I didn't need to add to my stress with heartbreak; so, I waited, and I am still waiting.

Psalms 37:7 says, "Be still before the Lord and wait patiently for him; do not fret when people succeed in their ways when they carry out their wicked schemes." God will give me the right man at the right time. We also see Psalms 37:7 say this: "....do not fret when people succeed in their ways when they carry out their wicked schemes." There are people who on the outside look like they are in love. However, this "love" you see can be coming from a place that is not love. Have you ever seen a person cheat on a test and end up getting a better grade than the person who didn't cheat and actually studied for the test? If you look on paper it is proven that they succeeded, but in all reality they did it in a way that is deceitful. Love can look like this sometimes; from the outside world a couple could look like they are in love, but how they fell in love is sinful. In God's timeline, I will find my right person one day, but until then I will not fret when others around me are finding love whether it be in the right ways or wrong ways; I'm not them.

So, if you ask me again, "Rachel, how have you not had a boyfriend yet?" I will tell you, "I am still waiting on the man that God will send my way, but until then I will be patient and continue to serve the one man that always has my back, and that is Jesus Christ."

Chapter 15 – I Am His

I have lived in Minnesota my whole life. I grew up in the church, and I have a loving mom who continues to speak the truth of God's word over me every day. I was also blessed to be able to buy a Bible and have one in my home growing up. Having all these things and being able to go to church and to read my Bible are amazing. However, these are not the reasons I love the Lord. These are all a part of my journey to getting to know Him and eventually love Him, but those things are not the reasons why. For instance, I love ice cream; it is probably my all-time favorite food on the planet. However, I don't love ice cream because of the milk in it or just because it has lots of sugar in it. I love ice cream because of the mixture of different ingredients that make ice cream what it is.

You see, if you take the milk out of ice cream, then you're just left with heavy whipping cream, sugar, and vanilla extract, which doesn't make ice cream. Our faith and love toward God is very similar to this. We need not just the church and the Bible, but the Bible, the loving Christian community, and the desire to love Him. I think it is important to note that if we do not have the desire to know more about God, then we are never truly going to love him with our whole heart. If we do not read His Word, then we are never truly going to know who God is. If we don't surround ourselves with people who love the Lord, then we will eventually going to become those people who don't love the Lord.

You see, I can read my bible one day, but the next I'm going to a party that I know I shouldn't be at; spending time with people I know I shouldn't be around. However, I read my Bible yesterday, so I'm fine; you tell yourself: I still love the Lord. When you do this, you are being a hypocrite. There is a Bible verse found in Mark 12:29–31 that says, "Love the Lord your God with all your heart, with all your soul, and with all your mind and with all your strength… and then it goes on to say love your neighbor as yourself."

Now, this is an extremely popular Bible verse. However, don't lose sight of the power this verse holds. Sometimes we hear one Bible verse whispered over and over us for so long that we forget the power that it holds; simply because we have heard it so many times. You must love the Lord with your heart, meaning loving Him so much that you are willing to give your life to Him. Now I don't mean to sound dramatic, but if you truly want to love the Lord, you must be willing to say, "Here is my life, Lord; Do with it what you please." Next is your mind, and your mind is influenced by what you see, hear, and learn from others. So, when Jesus says to love Him with all your mind, He is saying that whatever you listen to, read about, or learn about should be geared toward Him. Then He says to love Him with your soul, and your soul is both your heart and mind connected. So untimely, when He says to love Him with your soul, He says to love Him with our actions. Because when you combine your heart and your mind, they make up what you do; so, in everything you do, love Him. Once you are grounded in loving Him, lay down your life for Him, once everything you hear, read, and learn about is Him, once every step you make is for him, then you are able to fully love Him. Like I have said I'm 18 years old, and I have grown up in the church, yes, but I truly didn't start wholeheartedly loving the Lord until now.

I didn't start reading my Bible until now, I haven't even made it all the way through the first book of the Bible. However, God's Word is so powerful that even though I haven't even read the full Bible yet, I already have his love pouring out of me.

I have people ask me all the time, "Rachel, how can you have so much joy in the midst of your heartache? Rachel, how can you still believe in a God who you can't see? Rachel, how can you be so humble when the world is crashing down around you, how?" It is because I just don't believe in something; I love and trust in an all-knowing, all-powerful, loving God. Because when you are in love with something you can't help but let it consume who you are. When you are in love with God, He consumes you and fills you with this joy that overflows. So much so that others want that joy that you have. Then you are loving others, and then they go spread the joy that you gave them with the world, and then, eventually, the world is filled with the joy of the Lord. Isn't that amazing, isn't that just great? That one person who is consumed by this heavenly love affects so many people! However, this only happens when you love the Lord your God with all your heart, all your mind, all your soul, and all your strength.

I just recently learned something that blew my mind. Did you know that a cross actually is a symbol of what we are supposed to do as believers in Christ? The very thing that killed Jesus is the very thing that gives us a visual on what He died for. The vertical line, the one that goes up and down, is pointing up to God, meaning we are supposed to give glory and praise to Him. The horizontal line we take and split it in half. On one half of that line, we are supposed to love others, and on the other half we are supposed to love God. Jesus did not lie on that cross for six hours with nails in his hands and feet for us to give glory to other gods, meaning anything that we value more than God (our relationships, money, fame, the things we have, our spouse, or anything else we put before God). He did not lay on that cross so that we could only think about ourselves and not love others. He did not lay on that cross so that we could turn away from him, hate him, and not love him anymore when things get hard.

No, he lay on that cross so you and I could love him wholeheartedly; so that you and I could be with love himself someday. There is a sticker on my water bottle that is a little faded now, but I put this sticker on here to remind me of who I am and who He is. The sticker is in big bold letters, and it says this:

"I am the daughter of a king who is not moved by the world for my God is with me and goes before me I do not fear because I am His."

I love this sticker for many reasons, but one of the reasons I love this sticker so much is because even though it is a little faded, and even though it is peeling off on the edges; it has never fallen off my water bottle yet. You see, whenever I drink out of this water bottle it is a constant reminder that as I replenish my energy with the water that is going into my body; I also am replenishing my soul by looking at this sticker and being reminded that I am His. Out of everything that God created the sun, the moon, the starts He still looked at the world and said: "It needs a Rachel in it." How cool is that! On those hot days when I need water, He is there, replenishing my physical energy. On those mentally tough days when all I want to do is curl up in a ball and sleep, He is there, replenishing my soul. I am His, and that is something that can never be taken away.

Chapter 16 – God's Not a Genie

As a child, I always wondered what it would be like to be someone else. Or to be an animal or an inanimate object like a tree or a pinecone. However, I never truly wanted to be a tree or a pinecone for the rest of my life, and to tell you the truth, I didn't want to be someone else either. For one day I would love to be a bird flying around the world seeing all kinds of different things and flying so high I could touch a cloud. However, after flying for so long I would eventually lose interest and not want to be a bird anymore. I remember when I was six, I wanted to be a famous gymnast like Simone Biles; however, now that I think about it, being a gymnast is a lot of work, and I don't think I could handle all the training.

We all at one point or another wish we were someone else or something else; we are never truly satisfied with what we have or with who we are. Charlotte, Jamie, and I used to love the movie called *16 Wishes*, which stars one of our favorite actors: Debby Ryan. This movie talks about how Abby Jensen, (the main character) got 16 candles for her birthday, and if she could wish for anything, she has 16 candles to do it with. Which in my opinion, if I got 16 wishes you bet I would be using those candles. However, Abby quickly realized that what she was wishing for did not turn out the way she hoped. While I don't have 16 candles to use to become like Simone Biles, I can relate to this movie without having 16 candles at all.

Just like Abby, I could wish to be Simone Biles; however, I did not wish for the fame that comes along with being Simone Biles. Thinking about it, the public eye on you all the time is not something that I would want; I would want her ability to be an amazing gymnast, but not the fame that came with that wish. In the same way, we see the things that Abby wishes for are good in her eyes, but she doesn't think about the other side of the wish. She doesn't think about the fame that she may not want or the way her wishes could be affecting other people.

There is a line in the movie that I absolutely love! With all of Abby's wishes, there is also a fairy godmother that comes with those wishes. As Abby realizes that the wishes she is making are not turning out the way she intended them to, she says to the fairy godmother: "Your magic candles made a mistake," and the fairy godmother replies, "Candles don't make mistakes; people do." Once the fairy says this line it hits Abby, she realizes that all her wishes were not the candle's fault; however, it was her wishing that she was someone else, and in doing so, she realizes that her original life was the one she wanted all along.

We as humans tend to wish we had something else; we wish we were someone else, so we try our hardest to be that: Simone Biles. However, when we don't become that Simone Biles, then we get angry at God for not giving us what we want. God is not a genie; He is not a fairy godmother that we could wish for 16 candles, and He would give it to us. God is so much more than just a genie; He is a loving Father. When you have a loving parent, they don't give you everything you want just because you ask for it. They love you enough to say no, that is not good for your safety, so instead I will love you enough to go against what you want and protect you. This exactly what God does, He loves us enough to not be a genie in a bottle but a loving Father that will protect you.

So, the next time you sit down at the dinner table to pray or the next time you talk to God. Ask Him not to give you what you want but to give you what He wants. Setting aside your Abby Jensen's desires to have 16 candles and put God's desires for your life first. Because when you stop focusing on what you could have and start focusing on what you have been given; that is where you find true happiness. We were all made to be who we are and not someone else. So be the best you you can be, and don't worry about who you aren't. Think about who you will become by just being you.

Chapter 17 – Faith over Age

It was my great grandma's 94th birthday! My mom told me I should get her a present, and to be honest, I haven't a clue what I should get her. I mean, what could you possibly want when you have lived for 94 years? I would ask to be with the Lord, which is a very harsh thing to say, but truthfully, that is what I would want at 94 years of age. Imagine being on the earth for 94 years; your body is deteriorating every day; you are having more and more trouble getting up and out of bed. You aren't your young self anymore, and you can't do all the things you used to do. Who would want to celebrate a birthday that represented the older they get, the fewer things they can do? It just really shocked me that she wanted to celebrate anything. However, I honored her wishes and bought her some bracelets that had some Bible verses on them. I didn't know what Bible verses she liked, so I just got a variety of different ones.

"We loved because he first loved us."—1 John 4:19

"Be joyful in hope, patient in affliction, faithful in prayer."—Romans 12:12.

"For nothing will be impossible for God."—Luke 1:37.

"Grace be with you all."—Hebrews 13:25.

"The Lord is a refuge for the oppressed, a stronghold in times of trouble."—Psalm 9:9.

Once I had wrapped all the bracelets and put a bow on the present, my mom and I headed out to Senior Advisor. Which was a nursing home in Minnesota, it was quite well known and had a four-star rating, so a couple of years back my mom moved her to this nursing home. She is still a functional and cheerful old lady. She still plays sudoku, solitaire, and crosswords, and even plays chess with Richard, one of her friends who visits her sometimes.

My grandpa passed away a couple of years ago from cancer, and that hurt my grandma for a really long time. She didn't come out of her room for about 10 days after he had passed away. I remember about 5 years ago me and my family tried to help her get back to her normal self, but it just didn't work. Richard was one of my grandpa's close friends, he really helped her get back to a healthy lifestyle. She started to eat again; she started to exercise again and even socialize with a few more people. Once we arrived at the nursing home my mom whispered to me, "Don't say anything about Grandpa, Richard says she doesn't like to talk about him."

"OK," I said, nodding my head. We walked into the nursing home, and there were tons of residents yelling and wandering down the hallways; some of them still had their minds, but most of them did not.

We walked down a long hallway that seemed to go on forever, and then we stopped at room 208. Outside the door, it had little flowers and a giant Christmas reef hanging on the door. As we walked into the room grandma was sitting in her rocking chair reading, and as she looked up to see who it was, her face lit up. "Rachel and Miriam, what a surprise to see you!" she cried. "I have been reading all kinds of sad things in the paper, so it was a delightful surprise to see you all here," she said, trying to stand up to hug us.

"Mom, you don't need to stand up, we can come to you, don't worry," my mom said worried she was going to fall.

We sat down and talked for a good hour about all kinds of different things: what I had going on as I moved on to my next steps towards college, how Mom's job is going, the weather, obviously her birthday, and we even talked about her old dog she once had. She was fully capable of moving just fine; however, she couldn't hear very well. We had to write most of what we were saying down on a piece of paper; as I wrote everything Mom was saying to her; I wondered what it would be like to not hear? How did she feel every time someone was talking to her? Could she read lips? What was it like for your hearing to go away slowly day after day?

I mean, Moses was 120 years old when he passed away, and he led all of the Israelites out of slavery, parted the Red Sea, and went up to Mount Sinai to get the Ten Commandments. He did so much and lived to be 120 years old; that is impressive if I do say so myself! Second Corinthians 4:16 states, "Therefore we do not lose heart.

76

Though outwardly we are wasting away, yet inwardly we are being renewed day by day." I had always admired my grandma's faith; she used to be a kindergarten teacher, so she had lots of patience with her students but not only that; she had faith in her Creator, and she impressed that upon her students and me. One day she told me that she could see one of her students getting frustrated very easily. She asked the student what was wrong, and he replied: "I want to draw a bird, but my bird will never look as good as Jacks bird, why did God give me stupid hands, I can't even draw a bird for Pete's sake!" Before answering the questions, my grandma looked at this kid's bird and then she looked at everyone else's birds. She noticed one thing, they were all drawing the same type of bird, while this boy was drawing a different type. As his peers drew what an egal looks like he chose to draw what a blue jay would look like. The assignment did not say you had to draw a certain type of bird, but rather it was your choice on what bird you chose to draw. So, what did this boy do? He chose to draw a blue jay instead. As my grandma continued to explain this story something that she said intrigued me. "His classmates went along with the crowd, while he separated himself from the crowd and drew what he saw a bird as. It wasn't that God did not give him the hands to draw, God gave him the same hands just like the rest of his classmates. However, this fear he had of not fitting in, he blamed on the hands God created. When in all reality it was never the hand's fault, but it was the devil who made him FEAR, making him think it was the hand's fault."

After she finished this story, I realized that you don't have to be a child to experience this feeling of not fitting in, or the feeling of being fearful. I also recognized that in this story the boy gave into the devils lies and the devil used it as an opportunity for him to curse the very thing God gave him.

I find myself in this same situation a lot, I get anxious over speaking in front of big crowds, asking God: "why did you give me an anxious spirit, when my friends speak so freely with no anxiety at all?" God did not give me this spirit of anxiety that is from a demonic spirit. God gave me a spirit of peace, and the devil tries to blame God hoping that you would blame Him to.

My grandma gets it, she understood why this boy was frustrated and she also understood she was put in this position not just to teach, but to love the human God created. My grandma has so much faith in who her Creator is that even in these days as she gets older, and her body starts to deteriorate. She still will hold on to her faith and continue to nurse her faith till her last day on this earth. Once my mom was done talking to her, we headed out the door, and I gave my grandma a big hug. She held my face close to her face and said, "Don't you ever lose who you are in Jesus Christ," with tears swelling up in her eyes.

So yes, my grandma is having trouble hearing, and yes, her body is deteriorating, yes, she is not the youthful teacher she used to be; but even if she loses her intelligence someday, she will always have a heart created by God. A faith made strong through continually choosing Him day after day. This kind of faith will not only lead little boys to see the bigger picture, but this kind of faith will also outlast her worldly body any day.

Chapter 18 – Pursue Him

The goodness of God does not fail, but the goodness of people does. The faithfulness of God does not falter, but the faithfulness of people does. The power God holds will not disappear, but the power that people hold does. The love God has for his people will not change as we continue to sin, but the love people have does. Now, you might be asking yourselves where am I going with this? Well, as you can see every sentence has the words "God" and "people" in it, and it also has the words "does" and "does not" in it. You see, God does not fail at anything; however, people do, and that is a distinction between humans and God.

The wonderful thing about God is that even though we fail, He never does; He still pursues us. He still is faithful to us, loves us, is good to us, and never uses His power abusively. As I think back to the time when I was in second grade, I remember a teacher named Mrs. Tay's. She was a short dark-haired woman that was always ready to tell us when we messed up. She once said that one of my classmates was getting out of control in the classroom. So, that certain kid had to be moved to a different class so he could focus on his schoolwork. Mrs. Tay didn't say anything more about this kid after that day. She never went to see him in the other class, and she never chatted with him in the hallway. She lost all contact with this kid; she stopped pursuing this kid, giving him to another teacher to see if she could try to help him. As humans, we can do this; we can give up and stop trying to help someone.

However, the beautiful thing about God is that He will never stop pursuing us. In fact, He doesn't want to stop pursuing us. Mrs. Tay didn't want to help that kid any longer; so eventually that led to the kid not being in our class anymore. God sees us get out of control in our lives. He sees us just like that little kid in my second-grade classroom, but He is not the teacher. He is not like Mrs. Tay, He never will give us away, and He will never see us as too much to handle. He continues to chase after us even when we don't want Him to. Because this world has a God who pursues not only you but everyone around you as well. The good, the bad, the ugly, the pretty He continues to love you no matter who you are.

You have a God who is pursuing you in your past, present, and future, which for some people can be scary. *"God knows who I was back then, there is no way he could love that mess!"* Yep, that is right God knows all but yet He doesn't care how messed up you are He created who you are. He knew that you were going to mess up and that is OK! Because we as humans need someone bigger than us, bigger than the universe to see us for who we are and still love us. Mrs. Tay saw that little boy's mistakes in the classroom too many times and didn't want to help any longer. However, God sees us make mistakes 10 million times a day and never stops helping us. There is a Psalm that talks about God being with us and helping us in the past, present, and future. Psalms 139:5 says, "You go before me and follow me. You place your hand of blessing on my head."

God is always placing his hand on us and helping us along the way. Even when He knows the sins we will make in the future, He still continuously loves and cherishes us. I think about this a lot how God knew me in the past, present, and future, but still decided to create me! It is hard for me to fathom because I am human, and my brain can't think of someone knowing me for that long and doesn't just tolerate me but pursues me! However, I don't have to try to understand it because I was not made to understand everything about who He is and how He works. Because then if I knew everything about God, then He wouldn't be God to me.

For example, if I knew everything that was going to be on a particular test, then that wouldn't make it a test. It would just be like another review; just going over the knowledge I already know, in this way the test wouldn't be challenging me at all. Tests are meant to challenge you and test your knowledge of a subject. In the same way, God is testing us, so we aren't going to know everything on His test either. However, what we are asked to do is try our best, and by doing this we have to study and continually pursue our God just like He has pursued us. Read the book that He has given you to study Him and continually learn more and more about His character every day so that when the test comes, you can show Him the best knowledge you have. It is true that God pursues us before we ever even think about pursuing Him. However, that doesn't mean it is a one-way street; for example, if you are in a relationship and only one person wants to pursue the other, then my guess is the relationship is not going to last long. If we want to grow in our relationship with Christ, we first have to pursue Him. It won't be easy and you sure won't see the fruit right away, but over time you will get to know Christ just like in a relationship. You will start to fall deeper and deeper in love with the character of Christ. God pursues us not because He has to, but because He wants to. We all should take a deep hard look at our life; realize we aren't worth of this type of God who continues to pursue us. We are awful as human beings, but yet we shouldn't let that crush us. Recognize your failure, repent for the wrong you have done, and continue to do your best to pursue Christ. It won't be easy, and nobody said it was going to be easy. You will have your ups and downs and that is ok, because God knew there was going to be mountains and valleys in your life. But I want you to remember one thing, when you are in the valleys continue to pursue Him, because when you reach the mountain top people are going to see if you pursued Him or not. I know without a shadow of a doubt that when I reach that mountain top, I want to scream I know my Jesus because I pursued Him.

Chapter 19 – Social Media

Social Media sucks you in and draws you away from reality. This is what most of my older mentors said, but my peers all contradicted these opinions saying: social media is a way to connect with others who you normally wouldn't connect with. It is a way to learn about others quickly and easily. It is a way to share your lives with others. "Do it, get social media," they all said.

However, I didn't want to, or did I? I was confused about whether this social media thing was good for me. Jamie, Charlotte, and Eleanor had some form of social media ever since they were 12, while Mia got Instagram when she was 8. Jamie, Charlotte, and Eleanor all had parents who wouldn't let them have any social media until they turned 12. Once they were allowed to have it, they immediately downloaded the app, and within only two hours of having this app, they were already posting a variety of pictures, videos, and stories that they wanted to share with others. Mia, on the other hand, was a rule breaker; she has always kind of been this way, always doing the exact opposite of what anyone told her to do.

One day I was staying over at her house, and her mom told her to clean her room, and what did she do? She dumped the already dirty laundry that she had sitting in her room for over three weeks strait on to the floor. After that, her mom made her fold every single piece of clothing in the house for weeks on end. She would eventually listen to the instructions she was given, but it wasn't without breaking them first. A week had gone by since I spent time with her, and she dumped all those dirty clothes on the floor. She asked me to hang out again, so I accepted her offer and stayed the night over at her house. I saw that she had been posting a lot of different pictures of her in various locations, and I asked her why she was posting so much. She replied, "I got Instagram, but don't tell anyone, because technically I am not supposed to have it until I turn 10, but what's two years early, right?"

I just agreed with her because there was no disagreeing with Mia; we all knew that from the moment my friends and I met her. As I watched her scroll through this app that captured so many different people's lives, I realized she wasn't connecting with me. She was so engaged in what she was seeing on the screen that she forgot I even existed. Then the next morning I went back home after a long night at Mia's house, and I wondered whether social media is good? If it was an app that was designed for good or for evil? As I thought increasingly more and more about social media, eventually Jamie, Charlotte, and Eleanor downloaded Instagram, Snapchat, and TikTok. Now every single one of my friends had it, and here I was knowing full well what it is and still having no desire to download the app.

I wanted to go with the crowd and dive into the social media world. However, I felt this fear of what it could turn me into, hold me back. In some ways this was good, and in some ways, this was very bad. I had this idea set in my mind from the night I saw Mia scrolling through social media that it was a bad thing. The only reason I thought this was because it made me feel so bad to have her ignore me that night. I wanted her attention, and she was giving all her attention to this thing, this inanimate object. So, I did the same thing I did whenever I had a problem in my life. I went to the one person who knew me and knew the world, my mom.

"Mom, do you think I should have social media?" I asked her hoping she would give me a clear yes-or-no answer. However, she did the exact opposite of that. She said, "Darling, you get to decide that for yourself; you are old enough now that these types of decisions aren't mine but yours." After she said this, I was kind of in shock. Usually, my mom gives long and deep explanations on why or why not, something is the way it is. Apparently not in this case, she told me bluntly that it was my decision, and at the time I didn't like this. I wanted a clear answer, and there wasn't one. I didn't want social media to take over my life, but I also wanted to experience this joy my friends were talking about; when it came to social media. A few years after I talked to my mom about social media, I still didn't download it. I spent 18 years without social media and finally on my 18th birthday I said to myself, "It is not the app that is bad, but how you use it that can destroy you and others." Before hitting download I prayed a long prayer giving this decision that I was about to make and putting it in God's hands. Then I hit download.

By comfortably seeing what social media is, I have learned that there are good and bad things to everything in life, whether it be social media or not. There are always going to be pros and cons, but I have had social media for three years now, and I can safely say I am different, these apps have definitely changed me, but it has changed me in the fact that I can see more of what it is like to live in fear of what something can bring. However, now I see the fear turned into confidence in who I am and staying true to that version of me even when new things enter my life. I didn't let social media form who I was, but rather I let me form what type of light I would shine through social media.

I think it is so important that we don't look at one thing as a good or bad thing. However, we see something as a chance to grow and learn from our experiences. If I hadn't downloaded social media, then I wouldn't be able to sit here today and write about what it is. Because I wouldn't have as much knowledge as I have today. There is a verse in Isaiah 45:7 that says this: "I form light and create darkness; I make well-being and create calamity; I am the Lord, who does all these things."

Now, it might seem that this verse is saying God created darkness, but it is quite the opposite. In the book Isaiah, it gives us a beautiful picture of God giving us disaster to accomplish a greater purpose. God brings calamity to

Cyrus for the sake of His people so he can rebuild their city. God uses even the bad for our good, He wants us to learn from going through challenging times. We experience calamity and disaster not because God wants us to suffer, but because he wants us to see his light when we come out the other end of that dark tunnel. He wants us to mature and grow in our faith and sometimes we must do that by downloading social media and going through the hard things to see his faithfulness to us.

So, I used to think social media was bad, and now I see the light at the end of the tunnel. I see that there can be bad things that I may face with social media. Yes, sometimes I will have to take a break from it all, but now I know and have seen the choice that God gives each and every one of us. So, let the destruction of the city happen, but once it is all said and done, do you choose to rebuild the city, or will I fall into the ruins of it all? Let the hard times be hard times, but don't come out of those hard times not taking anything away from it. We experience hard things so we can learn from them, don't come out of a disaster by not thinking about how you can improve next time. God gave you that broken city for a reason learn from it.

Chapter 20 – Are You Letting Your Rainbow Shine?

What is a rainbow? Well, the dictionary definition of a rainbow is an arch of colors formed in the sky in certain circumstances, caused by the refraction and dispersion of the sun's light by rain or other water droplets in the atmosphere. This is why we usually see a rainbow when water droplets are present in the sky. When I was younger, I always thought it was so cool to see a rainbow inside of a waterfall or right after a big rainstorm. I used to play in the sprinklers at my house when it was hot outside, as I jumped into the water I noticed if I looked close enough, I could see a rainbow hidden inside the sprinkler's water. As I got older, I learned that a rainbow needs a white light to form. Not only does it need the white light, but it also needs the water; the white light hits the water droplet and the seven primary colors this light holds are dispersed.

However, there is also a crucial part of a rainbow as well, we call this the bending of light. When the light goes from air to water it slows down. It takes approximately 8 minutes for the sun's light to reach earth, but if there was water that went from the sun to the earth, then we would see it would take much longer for it to reach earth; approximately 11 minutes instead of 8 minutes. Since the light is slowing down in water, the beam of light is forced to turn and refract the light. The fun fact about a rainbow is that the light passes through water droplets that are round. If we didn't have a ground, we would see that a rainbow is a circle of assorted colors instead of an arch.

When God promised Noah that he would bring a flood to the earth, he also promised that he would keep his family safe. The rainbow was a covenant between Noah and God that he would protect them. Now the cool thing about this promise is that it wasn't only for Noah. We just like Noah see rainbows as well, we to have a constant reminder that whenever you see a rainbow in the sky, you are reminded that God will continually protect you. God can't break that promise just like you can't break a circle. This circle that God created will never fade away, and it is a circle that won't lose its shape.

Now, while I was on this topic researching rainbows both in the scientific sense and the biblical sense, I started to realize something very interesting. A rainbow, as I explained earlier, travels into a water droplet as white pure light, and once that light enters the water, it immediately reflects off that drop of water and produces many different colors. As I started to connect the two scientific and biblical meanings, I realized that God represents the white light, that he is the pure light that enters our body. Once he does, he fills us with all these colors. Red fills us with love, orange fills us with joy, yellow fills us with peace, green fills us with faithfulness, blue fills us with goodness, indigo fills us with self-control and forbearance, and violet fills us with gentleness.

Once we have that white light in us, we have the Holy Spirit living inside of us. This way when we go out into the world people don't see one color, but they see an assortment of colors. They see a new us, a transformed person and this person is only able to look so different than the rest, because they accept the white light coming into their body. This person is one who has those fruits of the spirit rooted so deeply inside of them. They have so much fruit in them that it overflows out of them for others to see. People see the love they show others; people see the contagious joy; people see the peace they have, to feel complete with who they are. People see their faithfulness, that even though they go through hard things they don't waver on what they believe. People see their goodness; people see their self-control to resist the things of the enemy; people see their forbearance as the ability to hold back our natural reactions and instead treat the situations with patience and kindness. People see their gentleness, in other words, the compassion they show others.

People see your rainbow, and they realize that your rainbow is something they want to experience. The other day I was sitting outside, and the entire sky turned orange after a big rain. However, after the storm and the scary lightning, here comes a rainbow. The amazing thing about this rainbow is that I was not the only one who saw it. Tons of my friends who lived miles away saw it as well. We might not experience a rainbow in the way Noah did, but we do experience the same promise that God gave Noah: that he will never abandon us, that he will protect us, and never ever send a worldwide flood to strike the earth again. The storm that you are facing may look different than the storm I'm facing. Just like me and my friends saw the same rainbow, we also were experiencing different storms at the time. However, we all have one thing in common: we can let our rainbow shine; when the storm is all said and done, or we could do the opposite.

We all make a choice every day to live with those colors inside of us or not. As for me, I will continue to let my rainbow shine because I know when that storm comes, I will not let it take me down but instead let my rainbow shine through those drops of water so others will get a glimpse of who my God is.

Chapter 21 – Who Are You Holding Accountable?

It was finally August; my friends and I were getting ready to go to college and move on from the life we had known for so long and step into something new. I wasn't ready to leave my mom, or the town of Rochester for a matter of fact, but at the same time, I knew I had to. I knew I needed to experience the world for myself. As I stepped outside pushing the door open, I could feel the cool breeze of fresh air and the sun beating down on me. I was going to go see my friends for the last time before we all went off to college. I was excited, nervous, sad, and happy all at once. I hopped in the car and drove to Jamie's house. We were all going to meet there and just have a calming and relaxing day with my friends. We weren't going to do anything big or something that would wear us all down; we just wanted to enjoy each other's company.

Once I arrived at Jamie's house, all my friends were in the front yard playing volleyball. My friends and I love to play volleyball; the funny thing was though, is that only one of us played the sport in high school; the rest of us just enjoyed playing it for fun. I jumped out of the car and joined them, bumping the volleyball back and forth. As we passed the volleyball back and forth, Mia approached us with these deep questions that none of us truly thought about until now.

"Who are you guys going to follow when you get to college?" We all looked at her with confusion on our faces wondering what she meant.

"What do you mean, Mia?" Charlotte asked, dropping the ball.

"You know, are you going to follow Jesus, or will you believe in something else? We don't have to follow our parents anymore; we get to choose what we want to believe in."

I was in shock not because of what Mia said, but because of the fact that she was right. We are leaving our parents and the beliefs of everyone in our town, and we could choose to believe in something else. We all had the choice to follow different gods or become an atheist if we really wanted to. This question made me think about who God really is and whether or not I truly trust him. Do I really believe that he saved us all? Would I be willing to go into college knowing what I know about Jesus and still hold on to my faith when those around me don't believe? I mean do I really believe that the creator can be man and God; and never sin? It sounded ludicrous now that I thought about it; to trust a library of different books that was written by all kinds of different men. How do we know they weren't making it all up? We all stopped playing volleyball and went inside the house. We all had that question weighing on our hearts, but no one wanted to revisit the question. No one wanted to face the dark fact that they could lose their faith in college, or they could fall into the pit of worshiping other gods. We were all afraid of what may happen to our faith.

While I was thinking about this, I came back to the story about Peter denying Jesus three times. Peter was one of Jesus's right-hand men. He loved Jesus and didn't believe that he would deny even knowing his best friend. However, the pressure to fit in and be like the crowd got to Peter. He denied even knowing who Jesus was saying, "I don't know what you're talking about." Then he went out to the gateway, where another girl saw him and said to the people there, "This fellow was with Jesus of Nazareth." He denied it again, with an oath: "I don't know the man!" (Matthew 26:69–75).

All my friends loved the Lord and wanted to keep their belief that he was their Lord and Savior, that someday they would enter into a better place than what they have known. However, Mia was right: just like Peter loved Jesus he still denied even knowing who he was. So that night we all made a pact. To keep one another accountable for staying true to what we believe, even when the pressure of the world may tempt us to ask questions about Gods existence. Mia said she would text Charlotte every night a Bible verse to keep her mind oriented on what really matters. Charlotte told Mia she would do the same for her. Elenor told Jamie she would call her every night and discuss the temptations they both had that day and exchange some ideas on how to follow the Lord instead of falling into temptations, and Jamie said she would do the same for Elenor. Finally, I and Jamie told each other that we would call every night and pray for one another.

We all were going to hold each other accountable, so when those temptations come to us, we have people we know; a friend who will remind us of what really matters. I found that the question Mia asked was scary when you are doing life alone. However, when you have good friends who will hold you accountable and want to see you thrive, just as much as they want to see themselves thrive. Then you don't have to be afraid of those questions because you know who you are following, and if you need a reminder, you have friends who will stand by your side and say: "Yes, this is who you are and this is who created you." I also encourage all who don't have those friends that will hold you accountable. Then work hard to find that community that will keep you on the right track. Whether it is friends, family, or coworkers, when you have a community that is on your side instead of against you; you might just find that life is much more enjoyable doing life with people who want to see you thrive, rather than people who are only there for themselves.

Chapter 22 – From Flower to a Field of Flowers

A long time ago my mom started a small clothing boutique in Rochester. It started out as the size of a one-car garage and was filled with major renovations that needed to happen for Mom to even open the business. She had little money, but she was determined to make this little dream become reality. So, a long three months went by of working, learning, and failing. Eventually, this small rundown building was turned into a clothing boutique; it is now one of the most popular boutiques in town. However, this probably wouldn't be the boutique it is today without my mom's hard work and faith to step into the unknown. At the time she didn't know whether this dream of hers was going to work out or not, but she never stopped dreaming, she continued to run after this dream even when everyone told her it would never work out.

There is a story in the Bible that is quite similar to this, starting in Genesis 37 and ending in Genesis chapter 50. We see Joseph go through some very tough times; to his brothers trying to kill him, by throwing him in a pit; to him being sold into slavery. As if this wasn't enough eventually, he gets thrown into prison. Then he was instructed to interpret Pharaoh's dream giving him the ability to become ruler of Egypt. Not only did he become the ruler of Egypt but also, he led him and his family (who at this time didn't know

Joseph is related to them. They thought he died in the pit) out of a famine. Eventually, he tells his family who he is and then watches his father die. He comes close with his brothers again, and then he comes to his deathbed. Throughout this pain, happiness, and success Joseph had; We see the origin of it all and that is in the pit. If Joseph had never been thrown into that pit, then he would never have been able to do what he did after that.

If Joseph had not been sold into slavery, then he would have never met Pharaoh and would have never became ruler of Egypt. Eventually helping the Egyptians and surrounding areas survive a famine. Just like my mom, if she did not start with a small building and built her way up, then she would probably not have the beautiful boutique she has today. We all have to start somewhere, and sometimes we start in a really good place; while other times we may start in the pit like Joseph did. Our success is not determined by where we start, but how we decide to crawl out of that pit and move forward. Joseph would have never been able to do what he did if he did not have God on his side, as he crawled out of that pit.

If my mom did not pray every night that her business would not fail but thrive, leaning on God for anything and everything; then she would not have the business she has today. God's timing is vastly different from our timing. However, that does not mean when things aren't moving fast enough for us or we aren't getting what we want right away, then we should just give up. Because God's timing is greater than our timing, and when you lean on his clock instead of your own, then your one flower will turn into a field of amazing wildflowers in His time.

We in our human nature want everything to happen fast. Especially in generation Z, my generation. We have grown up with fast food, where with a click of a button our food can be delivered right to our doorstep. With one search button, we can find endless information on any topic we want to know at any time. Within three hours you could be in Minnesota and the next in Florida just by clicking on the button to book a flight. All of these things aren't bad; it is amazing that we can travel in a quick manner. However, the result of having all these things happen so quickly, is now it's expected to happen all the time. In some cases, things won't happen fast. You won't be able to become an astronaut within one year of training; this is something that will take a lot of work and time. There will be times when you feel as if you were in that pit like Joseph. Your ability to persevere through these tough times will be tested. At the same time your ability to lean on the Truth will be tested as well. However, if you lean on the Truth, it will not only make the success greater but also show others that in His timing everything will become a beautiful field of wonderful wildflowers. These flowers can withstand anything because they were rooted in the Truth to begin with. So, whether you're building a business that just doesn't seem to be taking off, or you're waiting to find the perfect job so you can fulfill your dreams. Remember the process of growing a flower is hard and takes time. If you grow your flower in the Truth, you may find that at the end of your waiting season your roots are the strongest they ever have been before. Because you now know that you can withstand autumn, winter, spring, and summer. However, you only know this fact because you went through the prosses first.

Chapter 23 – Are You on the Narrow or Wide Path?

Sometimes I ask why when I should be asking how. Sometimes I ask where, when I should be asking when, and sometimes I ask for something when I should be asking for Christ all along. We've all had those days when our prayers are centered around the why. Why did you do this, God? Why aren't I seeing you work in my life? Why haven't I got what I wanted yet God, WHY? When we should have faith and believe that he will show up prompting us to ask the question, when? When will you work in my life? Believing that He will eventually work in our lives for good. We also have those days when we shouldn't be asking God to give us something. A spouse, a better car, money, but asking him to work in our lives so we may find our importance in Him instead of those fatal things.

We could choose to pray for the why, where, or something. Or we could choose to pray for the how, when, and Christ. My family, especially my mom, has put prayer at the forefront of her mind every time she thinks about the Lord. Every meal she eats, every time she sees that sunrise in the east and sunset in the west she prays. Prayer has been a big part of my family's life. I pray a lot; however, I never truly knew how to properly pray until a few years ago. A while back my mother had an uncle who was not a believer, and he never trusted in God. He never found the importance of believing in a God, let alone a hevan or a hell. He was a wonderful man, who was kind, generous, loving, and would always put others first, but he didn't believe in God. While he knew the rest of his family believed in God, he did not. No one in my family hated him for it. We respected his choice and loved him anyway. However, when it came to life or death, where would he go? What would happen when he dies, and could a good soul still go to hell?

He was told by countless people that Jesus loves him, and he still never found the importance of believing in Jesus. So, when a person is repeatedly shown the Truth, but rejects it what do you do? Does that mean that even though they are a good person, they still will be punished with the depths of hell? I grew up in a church where I was taught that if you believe and are baptized, then you will go to heaven, and if you don't believe and aren't baptized, then you go to hell. It was a very black-and-white way of living; there was no gray area at all. So, when it came to the day when my mom's uncle passed away, we had a celebration of life for him. We celebrated his life and the good soul that he was. However, this deep question weighed me down from the moment I arrived at his celebration of life till now. Did he go to heaven or hell?

As Christians, our duty on this earth is to tell everyone in the world about who Jesus is and what he has done for us. This way when we get to heaven we see as many people as possible. We are supposed to spread the good news to all who are willing to listen, helping everyone to reach those heavenly gates. What happens when you love someone so much, but they refuse to take the love you are offering them? What happens when the love of Jesus Christ isn't enough? I struggled really hard with these questions. Because death is something that we all experience but yet know little about. I grew up learning and hearing what Jesus says: "I am the resurrection and the life. Those who believe in me, even though they die, will live, and everyone who lives and believes in me will never die" (John 11:25–26).

My uncle died believing that God was not real; he went to his grave without the hope of going somewhere better. We see in Luke 13:23–28 the disciples ask Jesus an especially important question for not only their time but the time we live in today as well. "Lord will many be saved?" and Jesus says this: "Enter through the narrow gate, for wide is the gate and broad is the road that leads to destruction, and many enter through it. But small is the gate and narrow the road that leads to life, and only a few find it."

We all choose to go through the gate that is either narrow or wide. The wide one is what most of our culture today is choosing, simply because it is easy to go down. You just need to go with the flow, and you will continue down the wide path. The narrow road is much harder to go down; you must work 10 times as hard to travel down this road, resisting the easy flow of the wide road. However, that narrow road is what will lead you to eternal life with Jesus. This road will lead you to heaven, while the wide road ultimately leads to destruction and hell.

The church teaches that there are four things you need to get into heaven: (1) Being baptized, being born again of the water and the spirit; (2) Taking communion drinking and eating Jesus's blood and body; (3) Having faith that Jesus is Lord. The disciples even say that they ate and drank with Jesus, so surely because they have been around Jesus they will be with him in heaven. Jesus counteracts this and says the last point: (4) "Unless you do the will of my Father who is in heaven you will not have eternal life."

Not one of these four things says that you need to be a good person to get to heaven. We are all created good because we were created by a good Father. However, we were all given a choice as well; to do what we want with the life that God has provided for us. You must want to be baptized to get into heaven. You must choose to eat the body and drink the blood to see his face. You must have faith in him to feel that hope of going to heaven someday. You must do God's will in order to stand at the pearly gates.

Now this doesn't mean you have to become a priest to get into heaven. You can still do all these four things whether you're a priest, a nurse, or a mechanic. The good news about all of this is that Christ died on the cross for you and me; meaning he wants to guide you down that narrow road to him. No one person is too good or too bad to not be accepted into hevan. God is not playing games with us when it comes to going to hevan or not, He wants everyone to go to hevan. Jesus died for us a painful death so that we could have an option of being able to go to heaven. He wants us to choose a narrow road even though the wide one looks more appealing to the eye. He is also not leaving us out to dry, he has given us all the resources we need to enter into eternal life with him. So, did my uncle go to heaven just because he was a good person? The painful answer is no. However, I hope that this chapter not only speaks to the believers to spread God's word, so more will be in heaven someday. I also hope this chapter is a wake-up call for all those who are choosing to go down that wide path.

I hope that when you read this chapter you find what path you are going down, whether it be the wide or the narrow path. While also thinking about when you are on your deathbed, what path do you want to be on? As for me, I want to stand at the feet of Jesus and hear him say, "Well done, good and faithful servant. For the narrow path was hard on you, you still continued down that path and held your head high looking towards me."

Chapter 24 – Dreams

When I think of a dream, I usually associate a dream with sleep, an action that happens when you fall asleep and see a series of pictures connected to either real life or a made-up story. In most cases that is what a dream is; something that happens when you are asleep that tells a story of an event, or a feeling. When you look up the definition of a dream it doesn't just produce one definition though, there are several different definitions of what a dream really is. One definition is "a series of thoughts, images, and sensations occurring in a person's mind during sleep," which as I explained earlier is my view of a dream.

The second definition of a dream is "a cherished aspiration, ambition, or ideal." For example, you had a dream when you were younger to be a professional basketball player and on your 20th birthday, you got a call from the Minnesota Timberwolves to come play for a pro basketball team. You accepted the offer, and now you are playing for a pro basketball team just as you dreamed about when you were younger. This dream is where you have this thought of becoming something that you have always wanted to be. However, at the time this dream was so far away it almost seemed unreal. Then when the right time hits, you are a pro basketball player, and the dream that seemed so far away doesn't seem so far after all.

The last type of dream is a daydream. This is similar to dreams you experience when you are sleeping. However, they are usually more realistic than dreams you experience at night, and they obviously happen during the day. For instance, an example of a daydream is wishing you were in Hawaii dreaming about all the amazing things you could be doing in Hawaii versus you actually physically being in Alaska. This daydream is distracting you from your reality, giving you the opportunity to escape too somewhere better.

Unfortunately, I have experienced all three of these types of dreams. Whether good or bad, I have been distracted by my dreams. I have experienced my dreams come true, and I have watched my dreams fall apart. We as humans experience all kinds of different dreams, but very few of us truly act on our dreams. We see the basketball in front of us but never do the work to become a pro basketball player. We experience the fear of our dream not working out, so we don't even try to go after that dream we have. We see our dream as just a fictional thing that could never truly happen in real life. While others may make us doubt ourselves, telling us our dream will never work out. So, we should just stop trying to make them happen. There are so many reasons people don't chase their dreams, but what it boils down to is this. Do you have the drive to make it happen, are you willing to fail and get back up, and lastly, are you ready for people to doubt your abilities, but you go after this dream anyway?

Because chasing a dream, whether big or small, is not an easy task. If you have the ability to go after it anyway, despite what others say, despite the fear you may have, despite the fact that you might fail at this dream. If you can do all of this, while also letting God run your life letting him be at the forefront of every step you take for that dream. Then you will be amazed at what that dream can turn into. The Bible says we are not supposed to chase this dream we have alone but take up our crosses and let God lead our dream. God knows our path, but He also knows those dreams you have, because he was the one who put that dream in your heart. He knows that someday you want to become a basketball player for the Minnesota Timberwolves. If you work hard at your potential dream with God right next to you, you might just find that your dream has now become a reality with Him.

Before we were even born God knew who we were going to be. He knew that we were going to dream big someday. These dreams we have are not there by accident. God has impressed these dreams on your heart for a reason. However, we have to entrust that God will take care of our dreams, that He will take your dream and use it for His good. As I go off to college, I have lots of dreams of becoming an amazing wife to my potential husband, of having an amazing career that will fulfill me and possibly even having kids someday. These might not even sound like dreams to some who already have a family or an amazing career. That is because they have already reached that dream of becoming a mom or going pro in basketball. However, these dreams whether they have already happened or not; are nothing without God speaking life into them. If you have a dream, but it just isn't working out, I would like you to ask yourself this. Am I putting God at the forefront of my dream? Is my dream something that God would like to see displayed on this earth? Lastly, is this dream going to lead God's people toward Him or away from Him? As an 18-year-old girl, I have lots of dreams, but they are nothing if they aren't with Him.

Chapter 25 – Church

Church is a building used to publicly worship God. Church is a place for those who have similar beliefs to gather to do one thing: worship God. Church is a family built by the body of Christ. Church is the place where we break bread and drink his blood, to remember the sacrifice that Jesus made for us. A couple of these meanings of church up above are either true or false. However, before I dive deep into what it truly means to be a church family, I would like to give you some information on my church family.

I grew up going to church, and every other Sunday we would drink wine and eat the bread. This represented Christ body and blood that he shed for us. Every Sunday we would go to the same place for the same reason every single time. That one reason was to worship the Lord; to set aside our daily routines to take some time to reflect on what the Lord did for us and why we should praise him. When I was younger, I didn't have the attention span to sit through a whole church service, yelling and screaming so loud the whole church could hear me. When the pastor was about to speak, I would get up and run around the church during a service because I was five, and I didn't know any better.

There were many things at the age of five that I didn't know about when it came to church. Even now, as an 18-year-old girl, there are still many things I don't know about when it comes to church. There is one thing that I do know though. The church is not the reason you should hate God. Let me say it again, the church is not the reason you should hate God. In Acts 2:42–47 it paints a beautiful picture of what the church is. "And they devoted themselves to the apostles' teaching and the fellowship, to the breaking of bread and the prayers. And awe came upon every soul, and many wonders and signs were being done through the apostles. And all who believed were together and had all things in common. And they were selling their possessions and belongings and distributing the proceeds to all, as any had needed. And day by day, attending the temple together and breaking bread in their homes, they received their food with glad and generous hearts, praising God and having favor with all the people. And the Lord added to their number day by day those who were being saved."

As a five-year-old child, I went to church because my parents forced me to. Now I go to church not because I am forced to, but because I have a need for it. I have a need for a Christian community, and what better place to find one than church. This is where all God's believers gather with one goal in mind: that is to worship together and praise God together. It says in the beginning of Acts 2:42–47 that they devoted their lives to those who were preaching the good news, and they came together to break the bread. We as Christians come together with all different types of people with the same goal, and that is to worship the Lord our God. This does not mean dividing and splitting up when we disagree on something.

This does not mean just because someone doesn't relate to you that we can't be kind to them. This also doesn't mean the church is a building. No, it's a body of Christ, and in Acts it tells us this: "And day by day, attending the temple together and breaking bread in their homes, they received their food with glad and generous hearts, praising God and having favor with all the people." Every single day *together* believers in Christ gathered in their homes, and they broke bread. The church is wherever you make the church.

A while back I went on a mission trip to Belle Glade, Florida. We were instructed on this mission trip to help this church rebuild. They had a terrible hurricane that destroyed the building they worshipped in. It was a lot of work to clean this church up I'm not going to lie to you. It felt like we picked up trash for days. Putting up the drywall and cleaning off the debris that was near the church was not an easy task. Once we were finished it still didn't look like a "normal" church. However, once I walked into the building I saw one thing, and that was folding chairs. They were lined up like pews that you would see in a church, this place did not look like a church, but it resembled what a church should be. Believers in Christ come together with the same purpose in mind, to glorify the kingdom. Coming together, whether it be in a temple or your home and praising the Lord should never be looked down upon as not a church. One very profound thing I learned as I looked at those folding Chairs is this: Doing his work not for a prize but for a much greater understanding of what it means to serve Him and help His people; is something that is greater than any building will ever give you.

1. Church, a building used to publicly worship God. False
2. Church is a place for those who have similar beliefs to gather to do one thing: worship God. False
3. Church is a family built by the body of Christ. True
4. Church is the place where we break bread and drink his blood, to remember the sacrifice that Jesus made for us. True

1. Church is where we worship God, whether it be in a building or in our front yard. We can worship God from anywhere. Whether it be in public or be in private as long as we have people coming together to fixate their eyes on Jesus. True
2. Church is a place with different people, different beliefs, and different lives find a common ground standing on the firm rock of Christ. True
3. Church is a family that is built up by the body of Christ. True
4. Church is the place were breaking the bread and drinking his blood to always remembering the

ultimate sacrifice Jesus had to endure for us to be in heaven with him someday. True

The church is not meant to be a place where division happens. Where one disagreement divides his people and deters those who once believed to not believe anymore. The church is not about one person's opinion but a multitude of people resting on the opinions of God. We are not supposed to drive people away from church but accept them for who they are and welcome them into a messy family. A family who's broken, who all have their flaws, and yet a family who builds their foundations not on land; but eternal life. Because when you have a family like that welcoming you in, that is where you find the true meaning of what it means to be a church.

Chapter 26 – Honesty

Honesty is the best policy; or at least I thought it was for most people. I was raised in a family that valued the importance of honesty. "Honesty or truthfulness is a facet of moral character that connotes positive and virtuous attributes such as integrity, truthfulness, straightforwardness, along with the absence of lying, cheating, theft, etc." Or at least that is what the dictionary definition of honesty is. We all see the world in different shades of color. Some of us see the world through the perspective of black and white: the people we meet, the situations we face, and the things we have are either all good or all bad. There is no in-between.

Some of us see the world in a different way; we don't see one thing as all bad or all good, we see a grey area. Meaning we appreciate the difference between others and things without letting them separate us or break a bond between something or someone. How we view the world is important to those around you and to yourself. When I was little, around the age of seven or eight, I remember reading children's books that had a clear hero and a clear villain. Obviously, what the hero did was the right thing to do, and what the villain did was the wrong thing to do. These children's books presented stories to me from a black-and-white perspective. However, the Bible was different from any other book I had read. It portrayed a story that was not black and white, but colorful instead. Take Judas, for example, in

Matthew 27 he betrayed Jesus, and by doing this he felt so bad that he killed himself. Not once in the Bible does Jesus say to Judas, you betrayed me, and that was wrong.

However, it does present the consequences for everyone's actions, even Judas's. We cannot have a basis for what is right or wrong if we don't have a truth to back it up. If we do not have a line we draw to say: "Hey, this is where we have crossed the line in between the territory of right versus wrong" Then how do we know if being honest is the right thing to do or not?

A few weeks ago, my mom told me to get a job, so I applied for a job working at a coffee shop. I applied, and after a few weeks of looking over my résumé and doing a background check I was in—I got the job! I was thrilled that I was able to get the job and maybe make more money, to pay for things I desire to have. I arrived at the coffee shop around 7 a.m., and my shift was scheduled from 7 a.m. to 5 p.m. One of the employees trained me on what I was supposed to do and how I was supposed to do it while working at the coffee shop. The first day of training was very overwhelming, but after a few days of working there, I got the hang of it. One day I walked into the coffee shop, and it was complete chaos! Employees were running around the kitchen like a chicken with their heads cut off, and others were taking orders at the window as fast as they could.

After about three hours the rush time started to settle down, and my fellow coworkers started to clean up and get ready to leave for the day. One of the last things I had to do before I left for the day was take out the trash. As I lifted the trash, I realized something wet was dripping down my leg. The trash was leaking! I hurried and rushed outside, not only was the trash leaking, but it was also very heavy! I decided to just leave it there and pick it up in the morning.

So, I woke up at 6 a.m. and got ready for work. As I walked into the coffee shop, Amber, one of my coworkers, asked me if I left the trash outside last night. At first, I was a little hesitant to let her know it was me who left the trash out. I went on and told her the truth anyway, and she said this: "Thank you for being honest; a lot of people here aren't honest, so I appreciate your honesty."

At that moment I realized that my moral standard was to tell the truth and be honest even when I don't want to. Because my line that separates right and wrong does not start with other people or characters in a children's book, but it starts with God. Amber saw all kinds of people who had different moral standards in telling the truth or not. Some didn't tell the truth because their moral standard did not align with telling the truth. As for me, I want my moral standards to align with the moral standards of Christ. Because honesty may not be the best policy for your neighbor, but you don't have to align your moral standards with what your neighbors are. Rather, align your moral standards with God; because when you do that, you are not conforming to what your coworkers do, but you are rising above that: You are saying,

"Yes, others might not be honest, but as for me, I serve a God who is honest, so I will be honest as well."

Chapter 27 – The Phases of the Moon

Full moon, waning gibbous, half-moon, waxing crescent, blood moon, and toenail crescent? Wait, what? That is not a moon!

In fourth grade, I was taught the different phases of the moon that we see throughout the year. There are eight different phases that the moon undergoes every single year. As a fourth grader, I learned all about the moon and its different phases; we even had to take a test on them at the end of our unit. As I get older, my knowledge on this subject is waning a bit! I have learned new things throughout the school year, retained new information, and filtered out the old information. If I wanted to truly keep my old information relevant, I would have to refresh my memory on the phases of the moon probably more than once a year, for it to stick. Our brains are all different, and we all learn and absorb different information depending on what we feed our brains every day.

According to D News, our brains are capable of storing lots of information, from complex algebraic formulas to our favorite song we used to listen to as a kid. However, why is it that some things that we learn never stick with us, while other information we learn does? First of all, our brain is very good at remembering sounds, patterns, sights, and experiences you may have while doing or seeing a particular thing. So why do I remember ice skating as a child and not what I learned in politics class yesterday? Well, it is because when I ice skate it makes me feel good and happy; when I learn politics, I don't feel any emotions, except maybe boredom. I can remember how a movie made me feel but I can never remember what the movie was about; this is because our brains absorb the feeling more than what happened in the movie.

Our brain not only remembers how something makes us feel, but brain also remembers decisions we make that lead to positive and negative outcomes. I think we can all agree that our brain is very important; it is the central part of our body that tells the rest of the body what to do and how to do it. Yet God still created each of our brains to be different. Why does my friend absorb math better than I do? Why do I write better than my dad, yet he can solve puzzles way faster than I can? This is because the patterns that are formed in our brain are different, and we absorb different information.

I started to wonder why my friends know more about the phases of the moon than I do; when we all learned them at the same time and had the same teacher, who gave us the same test. After doing some research I found something; yes, we all have different brains and yes, it might be easier for some people to do certain things just because of how their brain was created. However, that is not the reason I don't remember the phases of the moon as well as my friends do. It is because my friends didn't let this knowledge they learned go to waste. It wasn't something they allowed their brains to forget over time; they let their brain absorb this information so much that they wanted to know more about the phases of the moon. So, they kept this information updated and increasingly learned more about the phases of the moon every day. We as humans were created by God, and we were all created differently; we all like different things and we all look different. Not one person is the same. However, we were not made by Him, to just forget about Him, once we learn a little bit about Him. He wasn't just meant to be something that made us feel good in the past but now is just a memory of a feeling. No, we were created by Him to get to know who He is and not only that but to keep learning about Him. Gain a relationship with Him and know Him inside and out.

Just like my teacher in fourth grade gave me a textbook so I could read and learn more about the phases of the moon. God has given us a book too. A book on who He is, what He has done for us, and how we are supposed to live. So, when someone asks you who created the phases of the moon, you know full well who created them and not just who created them, but how and why.

We are humans, and we forget things from time to time. We are human; we filter out information that doesn't seem relevant to us anymore. We are human, and we absorb different information than our peers do. We are not only human, but we are a child of God. We are called to not get complacent with the information that God has given us but to remember His Word, His promises, and His character. So how do I remember who created me, His promises, and His Word? Well, just like my friends who wanted to know more about the phases of the moon, they read the textbook. We should be feeding our brains every day with the Word of God. We should be building the type of brain that loves to learn about who He is and continues to know more of his character. Don't filter out God, don't let Him be just another boring memory: but a relationship. Learn more about him by reading the textbook that he has given us. Let what you learn about him mark not only your brain but your heart forever.

Chapter 28 – Publishing a Book

Some people lie, cheat, steal, and live in darkness every single day. They don't care who they step on, who they hurt, or about people in general. They are only invested in themselves and what they can get out of you; their one thought is me and me only. Now, I'm sure we all know someone who lives like this; we know that person that everything they do is for themselves. The center of their world is who they are, and what they can get for themselves.

A lot of people who live in the world today know that it is a fast-paced world. We are a society that values things like money, fame, time, and work. I see someone who has money, so I will try to marry them. I see someone who is famous so I will try to learn from them in the hope of someday becoming famous myself. I value time, so I try my hardest to not waste others' time or I'll try to get in as much work as possible in a small amount of time. Some people even think if I worked myself to the bone then maybe I would be recognized for the work I put in. Do you notice anything about these statements above?

They all have the letter "I" in them. We see that our culture is fixated on the words me, myself, and I. Everything we do is driven by that person in the back of our minds, *me*. Those two letters put together have divided us, hurt a lot of people, and I believe have broken the beautiful thing that God created man for. God did not just create man but also a woman so man is not lonely, so he could find another human to relate to, to be connected with. We were not made to divide this bond that God gave us and put the word *me* in front of it. God created us to make connections with those who are different, the same, and similar.

I want to tell you a true story about human connections, and how only thinking about yourself can hurt so many people around you. We all grew up in different homes, with different families and we all have experience different cultures as well. Our ethics and moral values are all different, and most of the time this isn't a bad thing. We can agree to disagree and go on our way, living our lives so that we don't have to converse with one another if we don't want to. Technology has made this quite easy; don't want to talk to someone? Don't answer the phone. If you want to talk to a certain group of people, then just don't include the people you don't want to talk to in the group chat. Want to post something about someone else without them knowing? Well, just make a private account.

There are so many ways to work around people these days. There are also more ways to do very bad things to people without them really knowing it, by just simply lying to them. As you know, my name is Rachel, and I like to see the best in everybody. In doing so, I get stepped on a lot, and I get lied to and hurt by other human beings. Not only will I tell you a story about human connections, but also how seeing the best in people who only think of themselves has hurt me. Before I say anything, I would like you to think of a person you trust. Now imagine this person going behind your back and lying to you. You probably wouldn't trust them anymore, right? Well, I was lied to multiple times, and I still didn't see the shadiness of the people I was working with.

Once upon a time, I wanted to publish a book, so I did what any other 18-year-old girl would do: I googled how to publish a book. As Google pulled up multiple different web pages, videos, books, articles, and businesses, I clicked on one of the first links and read what this publishing company was offering. The page looked legit, and in that bottom corner there was a chat box, giving me the ability to chat with another human right away to give me some more info on this publishing company.

So, what did I do, I started to text this person: whose name I didn't know, I didn't know what they looked like, and for a while, I didn't know what they sounded like either. Back and forth I texted this person on this little chat bubble gaining more information on this company. Eventually, they wanted me to call them. So, I gave this person my number, not thinking anything of it. Once I started talking to them on the phone, I could tell they spoke a different language by their accent. It was quite hard to understand them, but I made do.

This was the first call I had with this company, and this was the start of many to come. "Rachel, my name is Sam, and I will be helping you publish a book," the man on the other end said. It was very hard for me to understand them, but I wanted to publish a book so badly that I was willing to talk to anyone no matter what they sounded like. On and on he went about the process of publishing a book with this company. We discussed things such as the length of the book, if there will be any illustrations, how much it will cost in total, and so forth. We both agreed on that first phone call that the book would only cost $1,000 for me to publish. For the cover of the book, the rights of the book, the editing, and marketing would all be $1,000. That was the first lie I so easily believed.

After the call ended, they sent me some emails with more info on publishing with this certain company. The company was called Publish Now, (This is a fake name I will be using for the story line of this book, I will not tell you their real name for safety purposes). The first thing they sent me was the cover of the book. I didn't like either of the covers they sent me, so I asked them to make a new one. It took a little more work, but they were still able to provide me with what I wanted.

The next step was editing the information in the book. I had already had half of the book written, I just needed help finishing it. So, I sent them the book, and they edited the first chapter. It didn't look too bad; however, I did notice that some of the words I had in my book were still missed spelled; I wondered, if they were editing, why didn't they fix the misspelled words? I didn't question it for now, but later this would come back and bite me in the butt. It wasn't until I ended up spending $2,000 with the company that my parents found out about this place. Curious about what I was spending that much money on; they sat me down and talked about what I was doing. I finally told them I was trying to publish a book, and the company I was working with needed certain things to help me do that. I tried to explain to my parents that things such as editing and designing book covers cost money, so I gave them my card information so they could purchase the things they needed.

My parents were very skeptical, but we were excited that I was publishing a book, so they went along with most of it. I gave my parents the contact info of this publishing company so they could talk to them personally, just to make sure it was real and not just a scam. Nothing seemed too scary yet; I would write, and they would edit. Then one day they asked me for a $750 fee to pay for an ISBN number. This wasn't too outrageous for a couple ISBN numbers but for one it was a little pricey. After that payment, my parents called the company's number, which was not just one number but multiple ones.

At this point I had spent almost $4,000 on a book that was not edited, that was not finished yet, that was not marketed yet and truly was not sold to anyone yet. So, I didn't even know whether I would make a profit from it. $4,000 was how much it was going to cost me to go to college for just a year, but I had already wasted that money on a company, witch to be honest I didn't even know where they were located.

Eventually my parents called this company and found out that they were not ethically doing business right. They refused to hand over any contract; they wanted to sue me for not providing the money they needed after my dad decided to put a hold on my account so they couldn't take any more money. We stopped all communications with this company and changed my bank account number so they couldn't try to hack my account.

I was deceived by people who sounded nice in the beginning but ended up lying and stealing my money in the end. Eventually, I got the money back, and I was able to avoid being sued for something that I didn't do.

There will be people in this world who seem legit but just want something from you, and it doesn't matter what they do to get it. I was deceived and too easily convinced that this publishing company had good intensions for my book and me, I couldn't have been farther from the truth. I had never published a book before, and this company took advantage of that and used it for evil. They saw someone who was uneducated, trusting, and had money; they used that to their advantage. There are times when you should trust someone, and sometimes you do, and you learn later that trusting them wasn't the best idea. I wanted to do something so badly that I was willing to give in too easily to things that I shouldn't have given into. I was so blinded by the goal of becoming an author I fell too easily into the trap of the enemy, and his trap was to use other people to try to hurt me. I believe the devil tried to scare me into not publishing this book because he knew that if this book got in the hands of a nonbeliever, then they might just become a believer through the words in this book. The whole goal of the enemy is to prevent people from going to hevan. He saw an opportunity to do that through the publishing company I was working with, let me explain. He saw a vessel he could work through that was my publishing company, once he could speak to them then he could communicate with me. The enemy saw the blind trust I had for the company, and he used it as leverage. He thought he had a hold on me and the book I was going to publish. He thought he was preventing people from reading my book, but he couldn't have been more wrong. Because look at what you are reading now, the enemy couldn't silence this book, and he can't silence you either. Don't let the fear of the enemy use others to hurt you. God is so much bigger than the enemy and God wants you to share his word whether it be through a book, speaking or even just through a bible study, He will silence the enemy so His voice can be heard.

People will deceive you; the devil will trick you into thinking something is good when it is a scam. You will be hurt by those who don't live a moral, ethical life. However, God will never trick you into trusting Him just so he can get something out of you. God doesn't need you, He doesn't, but He does love you. Even though the world is corrupted with people online looking for only things that will benefit them. God is looking for things that will not hurt you but heal you. Even though there is an enemy out there working hard to take people to hell, there is a bigger God out there working 10 times harder to bring people to hevan. So, yes, I was easily deceived. I learned a valuable lesson about people, for sure. I learned that not everyone is good and not everyone does things for the right reasons. I also learned that trust is one thing that you don't want to mess with. It is very important, and the one who I can trust with my whole life is God. Because even though this publishing company and the enemy tried to take me down, God will never deceive me; He will stand right by my side and tell me the truth.

Chapter 29 – A Letter to Myself

I have one week till I move out and go to college; my life will change in approximately seven days from now. I will be with strangers in a two-bedroom dorm, and I will be paying for things that I have never had to pay for before. I will be meeting teachers that don't know my name, and I will be in classes with people who don't think the same as me; I will not have my parents backing up the decisions I make, and I will not have my dog to pet when the tears won't stop running down my face. Everything up till this moment in my life has been set before me by others; and in a way the things I have I never truly had to work for: I was given a car at the age of 16, I was given a roof over my head with no expense to me, I was given a free education at a school that provided the things I needed to learn.

Now, I'm being thrown into a world with people I don't know, with things that I have no idea how to use, I have the ability to buy anything I want, but yet no idea how to use the money responsibly. I'm going into a career that I don't even know will benefit me in the end; there are all these ideas of what college will be like, and the real fear is I'm stepping into the unknown. So, when "Rachel" can't think of what to do with all these fears that surround her every day, she writes; so, what did I do? I wrote a letter to myself, explaining all my fears, hopes, and dreams for my life moving forward.

Letter ~

Dear Rachel,

I have been struggling with what I want to do with my life. For a long time, I said I wanted to be a translator to help those who don't speak English to communicate with others better; now that I look back on it, I really didn't want to be that at all. I was using that in place of what I truly wanted to do, because to be honest I was afraid of what others would think or what would happen if I told people what I really wanted to do as a career.

I want to live my life for the Lord; however, I don't want to be a pastor because the church I grew up in didn't believe that females could be pastors. Nevertheless, I want to speak about my Jesus, not only do I want to speak about Him, but I want to travel around the world speaking about Him.

I also am in the process of writing a book about faith: I want to be a bestselling author someday, but the thought of becoming a bestseller is becoming bigger than the impact this book can have on those who need Jesus. I want to produce my own Christian music and possibly record an album someday; however, I have no clue how to create a good song, and even if I do create a good song, how will I get it out to the world?

With that in mind, I have an idea in my mind of what I don't wanna be when I serve the Lord. I grew up in a home where my parents made good money, and I was very blessed to have the things I have. I'm scared that if I do serve the Lord, I will end up not making much money and not being able to provide for my family. I also have been looking at "famous people," lately and realized that I want to live a life like them to the point where I was using these people as idols. I wanted the life they had so badly, to the point where I didn't see Jesus in them anymore but the fame, I desired more than their character.

I struggle with comparison, and to top it all off, I have dyslexia; I am one of the most least likely people to serve the Lord. I love Jesus, but how do I stop the thought of becoming famous someday overtake Him? I want to live a life where when I leave this earth people all over the world can look at my life and say: she lived her life loving Jesus. But right now, I'm scared of what my next steps are; I'm scared of who I could become if I do or do not become famous. I'm scared that I'm not living out what God has called me to do, and I was wondering if you had any advice for me?

I go to college in a week, and I really don't even know if I want to go. I got a grant that will pay for my college if I go into a certain major; I don't want to go into this major, but then I would have to pay a lot more to attend college. This is a very new and scary thing I'm stepping into, and I have asked God for signs, but nothing has shown up. I need guidance, and I was wondering if you have any to give.

~ Love you,

Dear future Rachel

Once I wrote this letter, I folded it up and put it in my desk drawer. I wrote this letter to get my thoughts out on paper, maybe it will help me find some clarity on the situation. The plan right now is to spend the first two years of my 20s at college; if I end up getting a degree or not, it truly doesn't matter. Even if I end up working at McDonald's someday and never do the things my heart desires, that is OK too. Because life is not about what you accomplish, but how you steward what you have with the time you have. So yes, I may end up serving hamburgers to complete strangers, I may never accomplish the dreams I have for my life. In this hypothetical situation to the world, it would look like I failed. However, I don't seek the worlds approval I seek the one who made the world, and if more people would go to hevan by me sharing the gospel through a McDonald's window, then forget the degree: I want the McDonalds window. Because when Christ comes back, He is not going to look at the things you did He is going to look at the heart. I want my heart to be ready for the Lord on that day.

Chapter 30 – I Must Decrease so He Can Increase

It was Sunday morning, one of the last Sundays at Autumn Ridge Church; this was the same church that I went to ever since I was three years old. What I mean by one of the last Sundays is I will be moving to college, and I will have to find a new church community. Our pastor, Pastor James, spoke about how we must decrease so He can increase; the whole sermon was based off of this topic. Pastor James emphasized on the fact, that we must let our selfish nature go, for God to even work through us; he can't do much with a human that is too full of themselves. "We must minimize ourselves so that we are not reflecting the world, but we are reflecting the one who created the world, which in our human nature is very hard for us to do." Pastor James explained. Then he went on to say this: "We are naturally drawn to what we can see, hear, touch, and feel; we are drawn to the world and our own needs above what is harder to see, hear, touch, and feel, and that is God. We are called to set ourselves apart from the world to experience something greater than the world itself. It can even seem impossible at some points in our lives to get rid of all this pride we have. However, it is possible if we let Him increase."

As the pastor preached more and more about this particular story in the Bible, I started to think whether I was really decreasing or not. He told us to turn to Luke 1:26–38, so as I flipped to Luke, I realized that it was the story where Gabriel the angel was sent by God to tell Mary that she was going to have a baby. Not just any baby though, but the son of God. I have heard this story many times before, and I even was in a play that was the exact reenactment of this moment in the Bible. However, once the pastor started to read this verse, I realized I physically heard the story; but it never registered until now on how important this story was.

He read, "In the sixth month of Elizabeth's pregnancy, God sent the angel Gabriel to Nazareth, a town in Galilee, **27** to a virgin pledged to be married to a man named Joseph, a descendant of David. The virgin's name was Mary. **28** The angel went to her and said, "Greetings, you who are highly favored! The Lord is with you." **29** Mary was greatly troubled at his words and wondered what kind of greeting this might be. **30** But the angel said to her, "Do not be afraid, Mary; you have found favor with God. **31** You will conceive and give birth to a son, and you are to call him Jesus. **32** He will be great and will be called the Son of the Most High. The Lord God will give him the throne of his father David, **33** and he will reign over Jacob's descendants forever; his kingdom will never end." **34** "How will this be," Mary asked the angel, "since I am a virgin?" **35** The angel answered, "The Holy Spirit will come on you, and the power of the Most High will overshadow you. So the holy one to be born will be called[a] the Son of God. **36** Even Elizabeth your relative is going to have a child in her old age, and she who was said to be unable to conceive is in her sixth month. **37** For no word from God will ever fail." **38** "I am the Lord's servant," Mary answered. "May your word to me be fulfilled." Then the angel left her."

The gravity of the situation that Mary is in is very important; not only to include she is carrying the son of God in her stomach, but she somehow must explain to her husband that she is pregnant without ever having sex with her husband. Here is the twist though, she must tell him she never had any other interactions with other men, hoping that Joseph won't leave her. She had to trust that God will help her and Joseph get through this and still keep their marriage intact. As I'm listening to what the pastor is saying, I'm thinking to myself, *I don't think I could do it. I really don't think that I would be able to handle the pressure of carrying the son of God; while also keeping the relationship that I have with this man stable. I truly don't think that I would be able to do what Mary did.*

However, if we dig deeper into this situation Mary is in, we find; the only way that Mary could have done this was to know who God is and not only know Him, but to have a long deep relationship with Him. That is the only way she was able to carry these weights she was dealing with. God could have picked any other Jewish woman, but he chose Mary. Why do you think that is? Why did he pick a woman who is not rich, a woman who is about to be married, a woman who is not popular? Why did God choose her? As I wondered about this throughout the whole sermon, my questions were finally answered.

God chose Mary not because of her earthly status, but because of her heavenly status. God chose Mary because he knew she had a relationship with Him. Not only did she spend time in the word, prayed and went to church, but depended on Him for everything. God chose Mary because He could trust her to carry out the task that would be overwhelming to most. Mary had so much faith that she didn't even question the angel, think about that! She was about to give birth to very the man who creator her and she never questioned her ability to fulfill this task. She never doubted what she was told, but rather asked for the process of how it would work. Then the very last thing she says to the angel is this: "May your word to me be fulfilled." Mary had to set aside her own worries, her selfish questions: How will I tell my husband? What will others think? What will my parents think? She had to set aside all those questions and have the faith to say, "May your word to me be fulfilled." Mary had to decrease herself to increase who God was within her.

I was not decreasing at all to the point where I had faith like Mary did. People did not look at Mary ever in the Bible and say: "Wow, thank God Mary is here on the earth to make God famous." Not once did the prophets or Joseph say, "Mary, God is famous because of you." No, because you can't have faith like Mary did and think of yourself, because selfishness or pride is not of God. When you let Him increase, He shakes off your pride, selfishness, shame, and fear. Then once all of those selfish desires you have are shaken off you are able to fully let God in; increasing His name, and once you increase His name then who you were truly created to be comes out. Because every single believer has Christ in them, but many of us do not shake off our sinful desires enough to let His light shine through us.

We have a light inside of us, but because of our need to put ourselves first the light is dimmed. We don't let it shine because we are too afraid to let go of the sinful desires we have. Once the church service was over, I thought a lot about what it truly means to let myself decrease so He can increase. So, what do I do? I post about Jesus on social media just to see what others would think. Within five minutes I got millions upon millions of comments negatively talking about my post. Within five minutes I was already thinking, *I'm never going to post about Jesus again, because the opinions of other people have shaped how I think so much to the point that I would do anything to get their approval.* I was thinking about myself so much that I was decreasing the light that was inside of me and increasing the *me*.

Are you going to let what the world thinks of you or what you think of you shape who you are? Or are you going to stand in front of the angel just like Mary did and have that faith to say, "May your will be done"? You must decrease your selfishness, pride, self-worth, fame, fear, and sin so that you are able to increase the volume of Jesus that is within you.

Chapter 31 – Rise with Him

I woke up, but I didn't feel like getting ready for the day; I didn't want to crawl out of bed, and I didn't want to do anything for a matter of fact. I was sad: I didn't want to go and be social today, and I surely didn't want to put on an act and act like everything was OK, because it wasn't. I was not OK for a long time; I would go to bed sad, and in the morning, I would wake up with tears in my eyes. I would see those who have smiles on their faces and wonder, h*ow does that work? How can they be happy in this world? This world is sad and depressing, so why try to go against that?* I told myself.

I didn't like my skin for a long time either, I would look in the mirror and hate what I saw. So, I tried to cover it up with lots of foundation, it didn't work; I still looked at myself like I was a monster that needed to be fixed. As I lived my life in darkness, I started to see that others recognized this pain that I was in; they saw the way I looked at myself like I was a stranger to myself. Now, not only was this darkness affecting how I saw myself, but this darkness started to affect those around me as well. They didn't like to see me hurt, so it would hurt them to see me this way.

I tried to make myself feel better; by telling myself, I was beautifully and wonderfully made by Him, but it didn't work. These eventually just became words I started to hate because I didn't believe they were true. I felt far from wonderfully and beautifully made by God, I felt ugly, and I wondered if God made a person shouldn't he make them look good instead of the way I look? I was insulting God's temple that he made, and the devil saw a crack in me that he could slip through, and he did. He came into my life and started to distort the way I looked at myself and the way I looked at others as well. This darkness that he was filling me with was not from my creator but from sin himself; I would look at other girls who used to be bigger and now are skinny, and wonder how their bodies transformed so fast? I also thought that if it could work for them, then it could work for me; how do I get skinny? How do I get Skinny? So, I did my research, and as I fell down the rabbit hole of Google, I found a way. It wasn't a healthy way, but it was a way to get rid of what I saw as ugly and turn it into beauty. The crazy thing about it was; is I could still enjoy the food I continued to fill my body with.

So, I tried it, I tried eating a bunch of food and then forcing myself to throw it back up because then maybe I would be skinny. I wanted to have bulimia; now to wish a disorder on yourself is very physically and mentally challenging. I would sit over the toilet and shove my fingers down my throat in hopes that I would throw up; it didn't work, so I tried a second time, a third time, and a fourth time, NOTHING! I couldn't do it; I couldn't make myself throw up; so, at night I would kneel in front of my bed, fold my hands, and bow my head praying to God to give me an eating disorder. I was so far from God at this point in my life; I was doing all the things, praying, going to church, and reading my Bible. Yet I was the farthest away from God I could possibly get. I was trying to force my body to do something that it was never meant to do.

Then one morning I woke up with tears in my eyes, a frown on my face and my body feeling physically exhausted. At this moment I realized that I did not want to live like this; I came to realize that I was not bound to this sin that I was letting destroy my life. I can be free through Christ, but first I have to let him in; God did not place this roadblock in my life, because he knew that I was never meant to have this roadblock (an eating disorder) in my life. He knew that I was created for a bigger and better purpose than what I'd wished for.

I was blessed to be able to have a mom who loved Jesus enough to give me a firm foundation on who he is and what he has done for me. I was very blessed to have this internal weapon, the Holy Spirit, to fight against sin ever since I was a wee child. Most people don't get this weapon and especially at a young age, but here I am with it, but I'm not using it. I was allowing the darkness to enter that crack in my body freely without even fighting back. How selfish could I be to think that I don't even need to use the weapon that God has given me to fight this darkness that I thought I was bound to?

How selfish could I be to insult the temple that God created for me? 1 Corinthians 6:19–20 says, "Do you not know that your body is a temple of the Holy Spirit within you, whom you have from God? You are not your own, for you were bought with a price. So glorify God in your body." God did not create my temple to be torn down, but to be built up. I was tearing down my temple thinking I had to rebuild it when I didn't even have the blueprints for it, in the first place. I understood now that I was not bound to this sin, so I started to wake up and realized that I am set free through Christ. For I am given the key to break these chains that once bound me. So, when I wake up in the morning, I rise out of that bed with not a temple filled with sin, but I rise out of that bed with a temple filled with the joy of being free. I open that Bible, and I read the truth. As I started doing this, I realized something had changed in my life; I found that by waking up with Christ on my mind I go to bed with Christ on my mind. Then the next morning I wake up and I am not sad, but I am filled with joy from the Lord. People don't look at me with sadness anymore; they see a person who is filled with joy, peace, and love that only comes from God.

Me wishing I had an eating disorder used to keep me bound, but through the blood of Jesus Christ I'm set free. I pray that everyone who is reading these words on this page knows. That you are not bound to whatever it is that may be keeping you in a state of evil; rather you are set free, so live like you are set free.

Chapter 32 – Who Are You Living For?

So, I think it is safe to say life is confusing. We all deal with situations that we truly wish we hadn't ever dealt with in the first place. We fall into places we wish we never fell into; we do things we wish we could take back. However, our life is something we should take seriously; we only have one life on this earth; we only have one chance to say what we need to say on this earth while we still can. Every day we have 24 hours to make what we want with those hours we were given. We have choices that we make in those 24 hours that we may regret and that is OK. I have things I wish I could take back, but I can't look back at the past, because I can't go back and do it over again. I have to continue looking toward the next 24 hours I have and make the best of those hours. I have learned how to live not in fear of what is going to come, but a life to the fullest with Christ, and here is how.

Steps On How To Live Your Life To The Fullest With Christ

1. I was not made to be afraid for the rest of my life. I was made to be fearless through Him.

2. You need change because although it might come with growing pains, we need it to learn how to adapt to new circumstances that God may have us step into.

3. Faith builds who you are in Christ. Ultimately you choose: Do I build my faith today by following him or do I not?

4. Life will fill us with what-ifs, but the ability to combat those what-ifs with an "I can" will strengthen your prayer life considerably.

5. We have many earthly fathers who will let us down, but when you build your relationships with a Heavenly Father, that is where you will find comfort.

6. We thank people all the time for what we can see, but when we slow down and thank our Heavenly Father for the things we can't see, we find our relationship with him begins to deepen.

7. Step through that door even though it is scary because you never know what kind of blessing God will have waiting for you on the other side.

8. When things change, and you lose people. Don't allow your heart to become hardened, because when you keep it soft, others will see your kind heart and want to be around a person who has experienced change but still can keep their kind heart.

9. There are so many ways to get temporary energy on this earth. However, the energy that will never run out

is everlasting energy, and that is the kind of energy I want.

10. Life will throw you curveballs. Knowing how to strike out, dust yourself off, and try again next time will get you farther in life than just running the bases like everyone else.

11. We are called to forgive others because Jesus forgave our sins on that cross. We are called to do the same even when forgiveness seems hard.

12. Be an imperfect Jesus because we were made for more than falling into the temptations of lying.

13. Love others even when they don't love you back.

14. The perfect man for you will come along in God's timing. However, until then you have a man who will continue to pursue you if you pursue Him.

15. God created the whole earth, but He also created me. I am His, and nothing can separate me from the God who calls me by name.

16. God was not made to give you everything you want, but to give you the things that He has in mind for your life. Sit back and don't use God as a genie but rather as a God who works all things for good.

17. Our worldly bodies may deteriorate, but our faith is made stronger every day by leaning on him. Our faith will outlast any physical body any day.

18. God knows we aren't going to know everything about Him. However, he does ask us to continually pursue

Him because by doing this we can be prepared for the test he may throw at us when we meet him face-to-face.

19. Social media is only bad if you decide to use it for evil. We have a choice every day: Am I going to let this app destroy me, or will I shine a light of Christ through this app?

20. Are you going to let your rainbow shine through the storm?

21. Those scary questions will come up when you begin to doubt your faith. But when you have people who hold you accountable for who you truly are in Christ, then you can take on any questions that may come your way.

22. When you grow your flower in the waiting season, and root it in truth, then you find your one flower turns into abundance of flowers.

23. Are you going to let yourself fall down the wide path that looks easy? Or are you going to choose the narrow path that leads to light?

24. We all have dreams and aspirations for our lives. However, the difference between putting God at the forefront of your dream and putting him at the back of your dream is crucial.

25. Churches are not meant to be divided but built up with the firm foundation of Christ; the only rock in our life that will never change.

26. Honesty is not the best policy for everyone; however, when you are truly serving a God who is honest, then you strive to be honest as well. Don't be honest because your neighbor is honest, be honest because Christ is honest.

27. God was not made to be filtered out, but to be a lasting relationship that you can have forever. Renew your mind daily and learn more and more about Him. He was not meant to be forgotten.

28. There are bad people in this world who will be used by the devil to deceive you and revert you away from the truth. However, we have a God who will never deceive us and always point us to the truth.

29. Your life will throw you in all kinds of different directions. Your four-year plan may not work out, but as long as you are living your life for Jesus, then you will end up right where you need to be.

30. I must decrease my own selfish needs to be able to increase the volume of Jesus in my life so others may see him through me.

31. I have to deliberately choose to rise with him, waking up with Him on my mind, because by doing this my heart begins to see the world differently, and by seeing the world differently my life begins to reflect not me but Him.

I was struggling for a long time on how to end this book. How will I close this book, I asked myself? What can I say to the readers to make them feel that they gained anything from reading this book? As I reflected on what to say praying that God would give me the right words to say, I came up with this. I have decided to end this book with a song. None of my family members or even friends have heard it before, so you will be the first one congratulations! I would like you to reflect on these lyrics and think to yourself: Who are you living for?

"I live for more than what they can see, I live for more than what they can hear, I live for more than this world I live, I live for you. Oh, Oh, Oh, Oh,

They try to break me, they try to crumble me, but I can't hear a thing. No no, I can't hear a thing. I can't hear a thing.

Oo ooo

Who are you living for? Oooo!

Ooooo oooooo

I choose to follow you. I choose to stand by your side oohoh. I choose to take your grace, your love, your mercy, your hand, and your feet let them be mine! Because I'm choosing to stand up and sing, my heart is all in. I am living for you.

Oh, oh, oh, oh, oh,

I live for the one who saved me

Oh, oh, oh, oh, oh, oh,

I live for the one who died for me, who loves me, who changed me, who rescued me! Who gave me grace even when I fell short oh, oh,

That's who I live for, so who are you living for?

There will be things in everyone's life where they don't know where to go, what to do? Or who to turn to when they need help? You will be completely lost, as I go off to college separating from everyone I know and everything I know, it is scary, life is scary, and you won't always have an answer for your next steps. However, you will always have a God standing next to you. So, as I go off into this crazy and scary journey; I am choosing to not look back at the past but confidently stand in the future and say I am living for Him! I pray that all my friends, family, coworkers, strangers and even my enemies may come to know the endless love that Christ gives. Because he has become my everything, and I couldn't ask for anything more but His love to pour down on this earth.

Notes

God's Not Dead directed by Harold Cronk, featuring Shane Harper, released March 21, 2014.

16 Wishes directed by Peter DeLuise, featuring Debby Ryan, released June 25, 2010.

Collins Dictionary s.v."rainbow" accessed October 20, 2024
https://www.collinsdictionary.com/us/dictionary/english/rainbow
Brock University Angela Evans, Associate Professor, Psychology
"When do Children Start Lying?" accessed October 23, 2024.
https://www.youtube.com/watch?v=G1A5J5UMqYo

Becky Johns. "How To Prepare For Skydiving 101: What You Need To Know" accessed August 15, 2024
https://www.skydivecsc.com/blog/how-to-prepare-for-skydiving#:~:text=If%20you're%20hydrated%2C%20you,jump%20if%20you're%20hungover.

Resource Of Hope Jesus "What Is The Vertical And Horizontal Meaning Of The Cross" Shari Abbott accessed August 25, 2024
http://reasonsforhopejesus.com/what-is-the-vertical-and-horizontal-of-the-cross/

Immanuel Bible Church "The Narrow Path vs. Wide Path" December 29, 2023 Pastor Jesse Johnson
https://www.youtube.com/wath?v=tkCYluplzJY

Collins Dictionary s.v. "dream" accessed October 21, 2024
https://www.collinsdictionary.com/us/dictionary/english/dream

Brian J. Trabb themelions "What Makes A Good Church? Reflections On A Church Called Tov" accessed August 30, 2024 https://www.thegospelcoalition.org/themelions/article/what-makes-a-good-church-reflections-on-a-church-called-tov/

Collins Dictionary s.v. "Honesty" accessed July 16, 2024 https://www.collinsdictionary.com/us/dictionary/english/honesty

National Aeronautics And Space Administration "It's Just A Phase" accessed July 20, 2024. https://science.nasa.gov/moon/moon-phases/

American Heart Association News "Energy drinks may provide jolt to heart, blood pressure" May 29, 2019 https://www.heart.org/en/news/2019/05/29energy-drinks-may-provide-jolt-to-heart-function-blood-pressure

About The Author

Rayanne Bedlan grew up in a small town in Nebraska. She and her twin sister were both born 3-months earlier than expected. At a very young age she was diagnosed with dyslexia and dyscalculia. This made it extremely hard to learn, but that didn't stop Rayanne from working hard in and outside of school. She graduated high school from Fairbury Public Schools at the age of 18 years old. She grew up going to Grace Lutheran Church ever since she was 5 years old. Immersed in the love of God from a very young age. Although she grew up with the faith rooted so deeply in her from a young age; She didn't truly surrender her life to Christ until the age of 18 years old. Prior to her surrendering her life to the Lord; she experienced thoughts of self-doubt, unworthiness, and even suicidal thinking. She states "Once you find the true freedom when you have been bound to sin for so long, you can't help but tell the world know who gave you that freedom. I was once a slave to sin but now I'm set free through the only one who could set me free and that is Christ." Her mission is to share the gospel with as many people as she can to let them know: "You are set free through Jesus Christ". Rayanne is not only a sister, daughter and student, but a child of God and she wants the world to know it.

www.ingramcontent.com/pod-product-compliance
Lightning Source LLC
Chambersburg PA
CBHW060831120626
46557CB00001B/457